# A FISTFUL
# OF WISDOM

# A FISTFUL OF WISDOM

## A MONK'S LIGHT MUSINGS ON LIFE'S SERIOUS STUFF

# OM SWAMI

Published in India by Jaico Publishing House

*Worldwide publishing rights: Black Lotus Press*

Copyright © Om Swami 2016

ISBN: 978-93-86867-28-5

Om Swami asserts the moral right to be identified
as the author of this work.

www.omswami.com

*This work is dedicated to my readers, many of whom travel far and wide to meet me in person. It is for you that I write and you inspire me to keep writing.*

*My immense gratitude to you.*

# CONTENTS

## MUSINGS

## SPIRITUALITY

## DEATH AND BEYOND

# FOREWORD

ONCE UPON A TIME A farmer lost his watch while working in the barn. This was not just any watch but his most favorite possession. His late father had given it to him decades ago. He searched for it frantically in every nook and corner of his barn, turning the hay upside down, but the watch was nowhere to be found.

Somewhat distraught, he was going to take a break when he heard children playing outside. He asked them for help and promised a reward of Rs. 20 to the one who found it. Excited, eager and hopeful, the children rummaged through the whole area, practically combing every haystack. But they couldn't find it either. They gave up and went back to playing. The farmer thought he would never see his watch again.

"Can you give me a chance?" a small boy tugged at his coat.

"I don't mind," the farmer said surprised to see a little contender. "But, other children and I've already searched everywhere."

"I know," he said. "I would still like to try."

The farmer had nothing to lose so he let the boy in and carried on with his chores in the field.

Twenty minutes later the young boy went running up to him.

"I found it!" he said and opened his hands to reveal the watch.

The farmer picked him up in his arms and asked joyously, "How on earth did you find it?"

"I just sat on the ground and listened to the silence," the boy replied. "After a few minutes I heard the watch ticking. The rest was easy."

We are desperately searching for our lost possessions, answers to the questions we don't understand, turning the world upside down only to feel tired after a while. And then we sit down, we wonder, we worry, we muse, we reflect, we accept, we relax. In that state of mind, life appears in front of us like the young boy and hands whatever is lost back to us.

Sometimes, the greatest way to search for something you want is to not search at all. When you just let it be, then you hear the watch ticking; you hear how life's bubbling over and you see the beauty in everything.

A young monk once asked his mentor, "Master, is it a sin to sleep with a woman in the same bed?"

"Not at all, dear," his mentor replied. "To stay awake with her might be. To sleep is okay."

Life is playful and it is demanding. Life is also a gift. A precious and priceless blessing. Why live it any other way?

Peace.

Swami

# LIFE

# The Puzzle Of Life

---

Sometimes all you've to do is look at the flip side and the puzzle of life turns into a beautiful picture.

---

THE OTHER DAY AT the meditation retreat, a woman told me that she had almost everything she could ask for and yet she was not happy. She had been battling a feeling of emptiness for years and had been unable to come out of it. She said that she had tried everything, including meditation, without any significant results.

"There's a constant void and I'm unable to enjoy my life," she said. "Everyone in my family is nice and I have no financial issues, but I just feel I don't belong here. I don't know what to do to get over my sadness. I don't know how to explain; I'm happy and I'm not happy. Life is a pointless exercise. On most days I feel negative and depressed."

"We naturally crave for a dessert when the tummy is full," I replied. "Human mind has an inherent tendency to ponder over negative thoughts. And by giving you everything, life has deprived you of the triumphant feeling of defeating your adversities."

"You mean I'm sad because I don't have anything to worry about?"

"Not to worry about," I replied, "to care about. You've nothing to care about. Find a purpose, a cause bigger than yourself so you may have a reason to care, to live and to grow."

I told her a little story as follows:

A father would play with his young son every evening after returning from work. Once, he had an important file to submit. He knew that he would have to keep his son engaged in some other activity so that he could focus on his work. While thinking about a solution, he chanced upon a large advertisement in the newspaper by an atlas company featuring the world map.

Carefully cutting out the map into tens of pieces of various sizes, he handed it to his son.

"Here's a jigsaw puzzle of the world map," he said. "We'll play together once you solve this one."

He thought this would surely keep the young one busy for a good few hours. The child, however, came back just after thirty minutes reporting that the puzzle was fully done.

"How come?" the father was curious. "It's incredible!"

"It was very easy, dad," the son replied. "When I started solving the world map, I found it utterly boring. But, then I noticed there was a picture on the backside. I started assembling the picture and the 'world' fell into place in minutes."

Sometimes, that's all it's about — the flip side.

We want to put the map of life together. We want to have it figured out, but it's not a walk in the park. Particularly because there isn't much to figure out, and to make sense of life is a taxing and tedious task. There's little fun in assembling a world map unless you are passionate about geography or puzzles. To stay motivated, we have to have something we care about.

The moment you find something that inspires you, life immediately changes from a boring map to an exciting picture; revealing its adventurous and endearing side, it shifts from being a pointless exercise to a worthwhile quest. Martin Luther King put it most insightfully, "Our lives begin to end the day we become silent about things that matter."

No matter where you are on the journey of life, there's always room for exploration, for excitement. Don't try to solve the world map. Instead, piece together the picture of your beautiful life and the rest will fall into place effortlessly. Find something you care about. And if you don't have a purpose that moves you, a picture that attracts you, that means you are not looking earnestly. No one is born with a purpose, everyone discovers theirs. A life without meaning is a boring one bereft of anything to look forward to.

———

A woman went to a doctor complaining of a stomach ache. After some scans, he told her that she has a terminal condition and has only three months left to live.

"Is there anything I can do, doctor?" she asked, deeply worried. "I certainly want to live more than three months."

"Are you married?" the doctor asked.

"No."

"Then find a philosopher and marry him."

"Really?" she exclaimed with hope. "Will that help me live longer?"

"Not quite," the doctor replied, "but it'll feel much longer."

———

The clock of life is ticking at the same speed for everyone. Yet it strangely gains different pace for different people. Some of us are watching thrillers, fully engrossed and engaged, enjoying every moment while some others seem to be listening to the weather forecast — flat and dreary, it can only get so exciting. What channel you tune into is entirely your choice. It's all there, you just have to push the right buttons.

If you have been waiting patiently and life hasn't given you an opportunity yet, then go out there and grab one. Opportunities don't really knock, they are created. As Buddha once said, "Your purpose in life is to find your purpose and give your whole heart and soul to it." The pieces of the puzzle will then arrange themselves. You will be able to watch every moment of your life unfold before you in utmost beauty. Every tick of the clock will lift you.

As you commit yourself to a life of purpose and happiness, your fears go away because nature catapults you into a much bigger play field. What you gain is a million times more than what you may ever lose. Anything that could possibly disappear from your life is not worth any more than pocket change for a billionaire. That's what purpose does, it turns puzzles into pictures.

# How Much Is Enough?

A beautiful story from the life of Alexander the Great
on the futility of reckless pursuits.

LEGEND HAS IT THAT Alexander III of Greece, popular as Alexander the Great, sent one of his messengers to invite the quiet yogi, Dandini, for a discourse and discussion on philosophy. After conquering the world at the cost of countless lives, Alexander was making rapid progress in his territorial coups. He had heard a great deal about the yogi. Dandini, however, turned down the invitation and chose to stay back in his hermitage in the woods. Alexander didn't take it too kindly. But being a pupil of none other than the brilliant Aristotle, he knew well that mystics and philosophers could rarely be lured or coerced.

He sent his helmsman, Onesicritus, to invite Dandini one more time. Onesicritus praised the yogi lavishly and offered him gifts. When Dandini didn't change his stance, Onesicritus threatened him saying Alexander had ordered his beheading should he disobey the command of the emperor. Dandini refused the gifts; unmoved, he told Onesicritus that he had no fear of death. Onesicritus couldn't muster the courage to kill Dandini, so, instead, paid his respects to the yogi and went back to report the incident.

Livid at being thwarted by a forest-dweller, Alexander decided to teach Dandini a lesson and set out to meet the yogi himself. As he, along with his marshal and the royal entourage, waded into the forest, a sense of calm began to engulf him. His anger abated as soon as he looked into Dandini's piercing eyes, but when the sage did not get up to welcome him, his fury rose back up once again.

"How dare you refuse my gifts?" Alexander asked Dandini. "They were smeared in blood," the yogi replied.

There was something in Dandini's voice, a chilling truth, a fearless conviction, that shook Alexander from within. Yet, he wasn't prepared to let his expression betray his feelings in front of his men. Alexander dismounted his horse and stood tall before the sage.

"Do you know who I am?" Alexander roared. "I don't think you know who you are," Dandini said.

This ticked off Alexander, who took the yogi's cryptic answers as an insult. Pulling out his shining sword, he raised it high in the air and brought it close to Dandini's neck with lightning speed.

"I am Alexander, the world conqueror," he shouted. "You are sitting on my land. Surrender or I'll kill y—"

"Your land?" Dandini chuckled as he cut him off. "The land belongs to no one, O emperor!"

"Before you, there were others who claimed it as theirs," he continued. "After you, there'll be others who will say it's theirs. All creation belongs to the creator alone, Alexander.

And no one has any right to destroy what they haven't created. You have blood on your hands. You may have a temporary claim on the land, but you have permanent scars on your soul." Alexander lowered his sword and uncomfortably adjusted his posture. Signaling his men to wait at a distance, he cleared his throat.

"The whole world is mine, Dandini," Alexander said. "History will remember me as the mightiest king! My men will die for me."

"What good is your ambition or their remembrance, O emperor? You drown yourself in alcohol every evening so that you may forget your sins. These men who surround you, they are tired of you. They'll give up on you one day very soon." "Besides," Dandini continued, "what will you do with the world? All you need is two yards; two yards long and two yards deep. That's all that will belong to you ultimately."

Deeply moved, Alexander put his sword back, bobbed before Dandini and left immediately.

Barely a few months had passed when his army mutinied bringing an abrupt end to his campaign in India. Three years later, Alexander died at the age of thirty-three in Babylon.

Even though it may seem that way, my focus today is not Alexander and his crusades. Instead, it is but you and me and our conquests. What is the sum total of human life? Are we to keep working towards eternally elusive and expanding goals? I say this rhetorically. At the same time, however, I do believe that in our continuous effort to be more productive and ever progressive, we tend to lose sight of the beautiful side of life — its simplicity.

Simple lives are beautiful lives. This is my view. A good meal, two ticks of laughter, a gesture of love, an act of kindness, that's what life is about, that's what simplicity is about. It's these small gestures, these simple moments, that make you feel complete, fulfilled.

And, simplicity requires great mindfulness and determination because it's so easy to keep adding clutter in our world of gadgets and devices. It takes no effort to complicate our lives in this uber-connected universe. Each one of us, an Alexander of our own domain, seems to have embarked on an endless spree of material acquisitions. By no means am I saying that you strip yourself off your wealth or that you don't aim for material growth.

By simplicity, I am suggesting that you take a stock of your life, mindfully. Concentrate on where you are and where do you want to be; what matters to you; are you truly living or just getting by?

Your perspective of life and your criteria of success will undergo a profound paradigm shift once you simplify your life. In fact, simplification of life is not a solitary event; it's a world conquest in its own right. Whether a glassful of water is adequate is not so much about the absolute quantity of water as it is about your thirst. If you are not thirsty, even very little will do, but if your soul is parched, a whole ocean won't suffice.

How much is enough, after all? For a contented heart, it's always enough. For, that's what nature is about — abundant, bounteous, enough. Always. It's simple.

# THE MONKEY AND THE COCONUT

---

Is it really possible to live a life of detachment?

---

THE TIMELESS VEDAS AND many philosophical treatises talk about detachment and equanimity for a peaceful life. Is it practical? Doable? On the subject of detachment, I once received the following comment (quoting verbatim):

> We have so many hormones, physical, chemical and biological factors (sic) working with our day to day psychology and there are gurus who say 'oh give up this and give up that...'
>
> Even they know that it is not possible [to] detach with (sic) your 'pleasure, taste and desire...' but they keep insisting on these things because they know that it is not actually possible to detach...it is part of our own brain and psychology...
>
> This is the centuries (sic) old trick that gurus [have] been playing with their followers to sustain their power.
>
> Don't be Fooled.

I hear you. You may have a point. Having said that, your doctor may ask you to refrain from deep-fried foods if you want to lower your cholesterol levels. They may recommend that you avoid sugar and go for daily walks, if you are diabetic. They may tell you that a wholesome diet and exercise are necessary if you want to lead a healthy life. Who doesn't like awesome desserts or yummy, deep-fried, culinary marvels? If they were not detrimental to our health, we might even be gobbling them up left, right and center. You are not going to die if you eat junk food all the time (eventually you will, though).

But anyone who's health conscious eats them in moderation; they exercise caution. They know there's a price to pay. And this is the key — there's a price to pay.

It's the same with virtues like detachment, truthfulness, compassion and so forth. You don't have to practice them. You don't have to give up your anger, jealousy, hatred and negativity (none of which is either easy or impossible). Just remember though, there's a price to pay. It will cost your peace and your emotional well-being. A true guru never dictates an action or a path, he or she will merely tell you what has worked for them and the rest is up to you.

Maybe some gurus unduly highlight your weaknesses, or maybe your truth is hurting you. Maybe a lot of them shamelessly fool people. Then again, there are many saints who have devoted their life to the welfare of our world. They aren't all cut out from the same cloth. Anyway, my post is not about gurus or followers. Instead, my focus in this chapter is on detachment and letting go.

Attachment is natural, even comforting at times, but as I just said, it has a price. If you are happy riding the emotional roller-coaster of life, by all means then, cling to your current temperament and feelings. But, if you want to experience deep and long-lasting bliss, there is much you'll have to let go. And, the foundation of letting go is detachment.

Unless you learn to practice detachment, it's not possible to truly let go. When someone hurts you, for example, you may say that you've forgiven that person or that you have let go, but until you spiritually detach yourself from the offender, letting go is impossible. Thoughts about them will still bother you, memories of them will make you restless and what they did to you will continue to haunt you. You detach yourself, and bingo, the pain starts to disappear.

Why do we remain so attached to our past when we know it brings us grief, you ask?

Let me tell you how they catch monkeys in certain parts of South India to shed some light on attachment.

In the olden days, monkeys would routinely destroy crops in the fields. The farmers, practicing compassion, wouldn't just shoot the monkeys and kill them. They would catch them, and once caught, the monkeys were taken to the jungle where they were set free. But catching them wasn't an easy task by any stretch of imagination. These primates were agile, notorious and aggressive. And if you think rocket science is difficult, then try catching a monkey (or do its mental equivalent — meditation). The farmers set up traps but realized that often the monkeys lost their toes, fingers or sometimes limbs in those traps. They cried out in pain and agony and the unfortunate ones were handicapped for the rest of their life.

The farmers had to find some way of catching the monkeys without inflicting injury. Clearly, it wasn't possible to drop everything and keep an eye out for the monkeys round the clock.

"There's a simple way," a wise farmer said. "I've been observing these monkeys and their behavior. We can catch them without hurting them."

To show what he meant, he cut a small hole in a coconut, just big enough so the monkey could slide its hand in. He then tied the coconut to a tree and put a banana inside.

In practically no time a monkey came, and smelling the banana, put his hand inside the coconut. But when he tried to pull out his hand, it would not come out of the small hole, since the fist clenched the banana.

The wise farmer began climbing up the tree. The monkey was its own hostage.

It could let go of the banana and take its hand out, but no, it held onto it tightly. The monkey made a fracas but the farmer went to him calmly and grabbed the monkey.

They hung hundreds of coconuts the same way thereafter and soon all the monkeys were caught.

The moral of the story: attachment is monkey-business.

On a more serious note, the root cause of attachment is ignorance. The monkey had placed a greater value on the banana than its own freedom. To let go of the banana, it must exercise conscious detachment from the object of desire (a banana in this case). You consciously detach yourself from something for a few weeks and detachment happens automatically. You quit drinking tea, for example, for a few weeks and the desire to have tea will go away. Try it to believe me.

Besides, letting go isn't as hard as it sounds. You let go of your thoughts, body and mind before you go to bed every night. In fact, it's not possible to fall asleep without letting go. The rejuvenation and peace you experience in sleep is because you let go. If you want a similar feeling in your waking hours, then sooner or later, letting go is a must.

Whatever it is that you are attached to, it will tie you down. It's as simple as that. Whether that's good or bad is your personal perspective. The prison inside our mind is built using the bricks of desires that are cemented in attachment. Awareness is the only door, mindfulness the only window. *Vairagya* or detachment is the only dozer to raze this prison.

If mind is a monkey, banana is desire. That clenched fist is attachment and the wise farmer symbolizes detachment. All climbed up on the tree of life. And, coconut? What's coconut? It's samsara.

# Is Astrology For Real?

Do nine planets, out of the billions in the universe, really control your destiny?

TENS OF MILLIONS OF people consult astrologers for various reasons. Out of those millions, a few thousand email me every year. Often, they write to me when they are worried about something their astrologer has told them about the future. And, generally, the same fortune-teller also tells them some *upaya*, remedy, like wear this stone or do this or do that, and the impending doom will be taken care of. Often (not always, though), the prescribed remedy has a monetary value too. This is where the astrologer profits.

If they charge you for giving you a remedy, they profit from it directly. If they tell you to do something where no money is involved, they gain from it indirectly by winning your trust. You think, *this is a good astrologer. He has no vested interest; he stands to gain nothing from it.* But, the truth is today he's telling you a "free" remedy, tomorrow he'll tell you a paid one. Or, to *you* he's giving a free amulet and he'll charge the next reference client you will bring to this good fortune-teller.

I'm not suggesting that all astrologers are out there to dupe you. On the contrary, there are many who are well-read, wise and intuitive. There are good ones, too, who genuinely believe in their systems of prediction. Unfortunately, that doesn't necessarily mean the system is genuine. Recently, a betrothed one wrote the following:

"We consulted an astrologer for advise on our marriage and were told that both our birth charts indicated that we would have serious conflicts and friction in our marriage, unless we changed the date and the time zone of our wedding, and also that my partner's life could be in peril if we married and stayed in India. Please advise."

Before I tell you what I really think about this question and the astrologer, let me share a little story with you from a Hindu text.

Once upon a time, a certain master who was a great *tapasvin*, rishi, with many powers, had a brilliant pupil who was only 10 years old. The master, who happened to be an accomplished astrologer, checked his student's chart and realized that he was destined to live only till the age of 12. Greatly disturbed, he set out to change the course of destiny.

Taking his student with him, he approached Brahma, the creator, urging him to grant a longer lifespan to the young student.

"I see your plight," Brahma said. "He's bright and can help the mankind. But, my job is to create. We'll have to implore Vishnu."

With a view to help, Brahma accompanied them to see the blue-god, Vishnu, who said that his role was only to sustain the creation and therefore, he couldn't possibly add more years to the student's life interfering with the wheel of time. He advised them to go to Shiva.

Both Brahma and Vishnu joined the teacher and his student to meet Shiva, the destroyer. The foremost yogin, Shiva, pondered over the matter and replied that his job was to merely destroy in accordance with the laws of nature. That it was not appropriate to use his power to stop the wheel of dharma. They advised the master to let nature unfold the way it was planning to.

The master, however, wouldn't relent and requested the gods to accompany him so that he could plead his case with the god of death. The holy trinity, along with the student and teacher, went to Dharmaraja — the god responsible for ensuring death of each living being. Meanwhile, two years had passed and the boy turned 12. He dropped dead in the palace of Dharmaraja — in the presence of Brahma, Vishnu, Shiva, his guru, and Dharmaraja himself.

The teacher was startled. "The most powerful gods are here," he said, "how can my student die now in your presence?"

Dharmaraja looked up, as if examining the divine record of the pupil to ascertain the cause of death and shook his head in disbelief.

"What happened?" the teacher asked.

Dharmaraja said, "This boy of exceptional intelligence was destined to do great things. Indeed, it was beyond my power to capture him. For, he could only die when none other than Brahma, Vishnu, Shiva, along with his teacher and the student himself, in flesh and bones, would all come together and visit me in my abode! It was impossible had you not looked into his chart."

I hope you get the idea. Let's gracefully accept the things that are not in our control and work on the others that are.

If there's any way to change your destiny then it is by working on yourself. Everything falls in place then. Gems and stones, totems and trinkets, and what have you, cannot change the course of time. If your marriage is on the rocks, then both partners have to work on it. If you are under debt, then you've got to cut down your expenses and increase your income. Wearing a certain stone or pacifying a certain planet is not the answer, if you ask me.

Besides, in the classical texts of astrology, there's nothing called *upaya* or a "remedy". Astrology is broadly categorized into two types: calculative astrology (*ganit jyotish*. IAST:*gaṇita jyōtiṣa*) and predictive astrology (*phalit jyotish*. IAST: *phalita jyōtiṣa*).

Calculative or computational astrology is a branch of astronomy that is primarily concerned with the movement of planets and stars. Predictive astrology is about the impact of such movements on you as an individual. There are no "*upayas*" in either of them.

There is nothing called 'if you do this or that, then you could avoid such-and-such incident'. (I say this based on two things — one, there's not a classical text on astrology that I haven't read. And, two, for many years, I professionally practiced astrology.)

Does that mean you should discard every solution prescribed by an astrologer? I'm not saying there's no truth to astrology. I'm only suggesting that remedies etcetera are all fluff. Think of them as placebo. Use it only for your psychological advantage. It doesn't have anything else to offer. And, let me tell you my simple principle. If anyone ever creates fear in you, be that person an expert astrologer, religious authority, preacher, or swami, it's a good time to abandon him. It is so easy to bank on fears. For your own good, if you wish to lead a life of freedom, don't give anyone the right to instill fear in you, in any which way.

If you have read my memoir, then you would know what I really think about astrology. Let me sum it up for you, nevertheless: I have never consulted astrology before taking any (major or minor) decisions in my life, whether starting or naming a business, buying a house or moving to a new country, investing in a company or embarking on a new journey. I just did what suited my schedule. I only consult the lunar calendar for some of my spiritual practices to honor certain traditions.

If astrology could solve your problems, why would an astrologer's life have any problems at all? Why would they fall ill or have wayward children? Why would they struggle financially or go through divorces? Something for you to think about.

Do you think that the world's most powerful, richest people, the greatest minds, inventors, philosophers, scientists, entrepreneurs, etc., went around consulting astrologers or fortune-tellers? Please wake up and look within you for the answers. Take control of your time and act accordingly. That's all that matters at the end of the day.

Have faith in yourself, in your god. Do the right thing, make the right choices, be compassionate and don't give up. You won't have to worry about astrology then. Instead, you'll carve your way through adversities and obstacles like a river moving through earth and stones.

# A Moral Dilemma

---

Can you lead your life in absolute black or white?
Probably not. But you can have your principles.

---

SOME QUESTIONS HAVE NO answers, many questions, in fact, have no absolute answers. The other day, a young physician came to the ashram. Let's call her Anu. She was rather depressed because of the situation at work. Working as a doctor for an autonomous body in the armed forces, Anu had to dispense fake medicines. Her patients are the defense personnel — the people protecting the country. And, they are being given fake medicines? Perhaps, the downfall of a nation couldn't be any worse. Anyway, I'm not an umpire of morality or a political writer. Instead, I wish to take the spiritual view in all this.

"Did you report the matter to your senior?" I said.

"Yes, Swami," Anu said, "they asked me not to worry. 'These things happen', they said. But, my conscience is not allowing me to continue. I'm giving my patients phoney pills and I know they won't be cured. I want to quit my job but my family wants me to continue since it's a government job with many perks and benefits, including pension."

"Don't just quit," I said, "blow the whistle.

If you quit, the problem will continue."

"But, I've only told you one of the problems," she said. "They are also taking kickbacks and commissions from pathology labs where patients are often referred to for tests. Everyone is corrupt. If I report it to the Commanding Officer, who knows what all I may have to go through? Further, all my doctor friends who are working in other organizations tell me that I'm being pedantic. They tell me that I'm oversensitive. It's a common practice at their workplace, too, they tell me."

"Taking commissions may just be a malpractice, but giving fake medicines is a downright crime. It's a crime in ethical, moral and legal sense. It's a crime against humanity. Silence is not always golden, Anu. Silence encourages the criminal. If you keep quiet, you'll become an ancillary to this misdeed."

"But, even if I report, Swami, they may do something real bad to me. Who knows, I may even be fired, whereas everything will go back to the way it was at their end. Oh, I'm so confused. I wish my family understood my quandary, I would have felt a whole lot better."

Her dilemma was: whether anything would change at all, even if she blew the whistle, and, if it was worth risking everything. I asked Anu to write down her principles, to write down what she stood for, and live accordingly. Her situation is a complicated one; her questions are valid. She has to choose whether she wants to continue with a burden on her conscience hoping one day she won't feel bad about it anymore, or, expose the wrong and put up with the consequences that could range from a suspension to anything unimaginable. Meanwhile, innocent patients will continue to suffer.

I don't believe morality is absolute, but when you violate your own principles, you place on yourself the same burden as an immoral act. You can't escape from yourself. You can only forgive yourself if you don't repeat it. I always encourage everyone to write down their principles — their top three principles. It always helps to know what we stand for. Decision-making becomes somewhat easier then.

Mulla Nasruddin was the magistrate in a local court. Once, the plaintiffs presented their side of the case and Mulla announced a short recess. Immediately upon his return, he gave a judgment in favor of the complainant.

"But, you haven't even heard our argument!" cried the defense counsel.

"Be quiet," said Mulla. "I've already made up my mind after hearing the plaint. Hearing your plea now will only add to my confusion."

The truth is, life will confuse you. You will have to make choices, make decisions. You will need to make up your mind. There's little wisdom in putting it off. The course of history was changed by those who challenged the 'common practices', who refused to withstand the oppression, who decided to stand up, and not by those who kept quiet. Nothing changes unless we act on it.

A noble life may have its share of stresses and challenges, but it does bestow inner peace and extraordinary strength. There's no room for depression in it. Everyone has to face difficult situations in life. And there comes a time when you can't delay a decision any further, when you must pick a side. At that time, if you are confused, find a peaceful spot and write down what matters to you in your life. Thereafter, make a choice that supports your principles and your priorities. Obstacles will become gratifying challenges, and the pursuit will become a fulfilling journey and your life will gain a new meaning then.

When you take up a cause bigger than yourself, the whole universe summons itself to be at your feet, at your disposal. This is the irrefutable law of nature.

# ARE YOU HURTING LIFE?

Learn to love life for what it is, for every bird sings a different song.

LET ME BEGIN FROM the beginning, with a story from the life of Buddha, the Buddha, who was once known as Prince Siddhartha before he renounced the material world.

Siddhartha and his cousin Devadutta planned to spend a day in the woods, resting under shady trees, playing in the pond and getting pampered by attendants and maids. A royal entourage was arranged for their comfort and safety. Devadutta had carried his bow and arrow along even though they had agreed not to hunt.

While they lay near a natural pool, a swan landed nearby. Devadutta saw a golden opportunity and immediately strung his bow and aimed at the bird. Siddhartha tried to stop him, but he was adamant. A few moments passed and upon hearing the commotion, the swan took flight. Devadutta was a good archer (unfortunately) and he shot his arrow. It struck the target. Seeing the bird fall, Siddhartha leapt and strode towards it.

Miraculously, the swan was still alive. But it was going limp fast as life was fleeing out of the poor bird. Its eyes were closing, its wound was bloody. Gently, the prince pulled out the arrow and squeezed cool juice of some leaves on the wound to stop the bleeding. He called one of the physicians in the entourage to attend to the bird and applied medicinal herbs on the swan with his tender hands.

The frightened bird began to feel at ease as it slightly fluttered its wings. It was in much pain to fly away, though. It lay there resting in Siddhartha's delicate hands. Devadutta didn't take it too kindly and felt robbed of his game.

"Give it to me!" he said to Siddhartha. "I shot it."

"No way, Devadutta," the prince replied. "I saved it."

"That's ridiculous," he yelled. "It's my bird, I brought it down with my arrows."

"Had you killed it, it would have been yours," Siddhartha said snuggling the swan, "but since it's alive, it belongs to me."

When the argument couldn't be settled, they consulted one of the king's ministers, who was a member of the royal escort. He suggested that a hermit, who lived in the woods nearby, was in a better position to give a verdict on the matter. As was the custom, the boys took offerings of fruits and flowers, bowed before the sage and presented their case.

"There is no confusion," the sage concluded. "A life belongs to the one who tries to save it. It cannot belong to the one who hurts it." "Therefore," he added, "the swan belongs to Siddhartha."

It's a simple story, but then again, wisdom lives in simplicity. In fact, it only lives in simplicity. Wise people are simple people. Personally, I find that the ultimate wisdom required for leading a beautiful life, a fulfilling and meaningful life, is shining majestically like a crowned jewel in our story. Here, in one sentence:

Life belongs to those who love it.

You protect what you love, so you naturally try to save what you love. If you hurt life, it stops belonging to you; it ceases to be *your* life. If given the choice, who do you think the swan would like to be with — Devadutta or Siddhartha? The bird would always be happier with Siddhartha, it would want to live with him because the prince tried to protect him.

Similarly, your life has a life of its own. If you love it, value it, protect it, it would want to be with you. It will become yours. But if you are going to hurt it, it will fly away from you, far, far away. Be kind, be gentle like the prince in our story and the swan of life will come alive in your hands.

You feel hurt when the other person doesn't appreciate your efforts; life is hurt, too, when you keep on resisting rather than appreciating what it's doing for you.

Life is frightened and hurt when you shoot arrows of jealousy, complaints and selfishness. Every time that happens, it distances itself from you. And, when your own life moves away from you, no one or nothing in the world can make you happy. Not for long anyway. By life, I'm not talking about the physical breath, but the essence of life that is, a sense of peace and bliss. No point in mistreating or neglecting your life, because nothing hurts like neglect.

An overseas visitor met with a Zen monk, who offered him tea. The handle of the tiny cup, paper thin, broke as soon as the visitor grabbed it.

"Why do you make your cups so delicate?" he asked the monk a little frustrated and embarrassed.

"It's not that the cups are delicate," the monk replied while sipping his tea, "you don't know how to handle it."

It's all about how you handle life as opposed to how your life ought to be. Life is what it is. If you deal with it compassionately, gratefully, delicately, you will discover that it's every bit beautiful, that it belongs to you wholeheartedly.

Learn to love life for what it is, for every bird sings a different song. Learn to listen to it and appreciate it. It's funny but true that when you start adjusting around what life has planned for you, life starts to move according to you. If you keep hurting it and battling with it, life will ignore you completely and start to distance itself from you.

As I said earlier, you feed life, love it, protect it and it'll belong to you. It will move according to your command then.

The answer to the question, "Why are you hurting me, Life?" begins with the question, "Why are you hurting life?"

Don't hurt what you want to keep. If you want to keep, that is.

# Living In Conflict

Make sure the light you see at the end of the tunnel is not an oncoming train. Life is synonymous with conflicts.

THERE IS A FAMOUS saying: what doesn't kill you, makes you stronger. It is true in most cases, except when you are really hurt and the damage is beyond repair. There is no charm, no hope, no promise, no light. I get scores of emails where people have been abandoned, betrayed, wronged, sometimes laid off, demoted, deprived, denied and what have you. Some manage to pick themselves up and move on, many are never healed. In majority of such emails, they are looking for answers. They write to me asking what bad karma did they do, where did they go wrong, why did it happen to them. The truth is, it is not always about what you did or didn't, sometimes, it is just about the other person, their own priorities.

When you are tired of fire-fighting, when life constantly keeps on knocking you down, when your path continues to get blocked, it often means it is a calling. A calling for change. If you resist or ignore change at that moment, the next blow will be more like a knockout punch. At that time, it will not make you strong. Instead, it may cause irreversible damage. We don't want you to get hurt beyond restoration. It is better to gain your strength from inner peace than external resistance. You cannot change the economy, the government, your employer, your boss, your industry. It is childish to expect them to treat you with love. It is unrealistic to expect life to always handle you the way you like.

The flight attendant asked a passenger aboard, "Would you like to have dinner?"

"What are my choices?" he said.

"Yes or no," she replied instantly.

Sometimes, the only choice you have is a Yes or a No. If you are going to keep waiting for better options, if you continue to oppose, you may miss the most significant and defining moments of your life. There is only so much analysis and thinking you can do. When you reach a stage where further thinking yields nothing more than a headache, when your mind goes numb, when understanding ends, it does not necessarily mean that the conclusion you have is the answer you have been looking for, or that there is no answer at all. In the words of American theologian and mystic Thomas Merton, "It is simply a reminder to stop thinking and start looking. Perhaps there is nothing to figure out after all; perhaps we only need to wake up."

Ultimately, everything boils down to your response to any situation. Give a thought to how you want to respond, make a choice and put it to action. If your response does not change, the outcome will remain the same, too. Act!

English poet William Henley penned down a beautiful poem, *Invictus*. It has been one of my favorite poems since childhood. I quote it here:

Out of the night that covers me,
Black as the Pit from pole to pole,
I thank whatever gods may be
For my unconquerable soul.

In the fell clutch of circumstance
I have not winced nor cried aloud.
Under the bludgeonings of chance
My head is bloody, but unbowed.

Beyond this place of wrath and tears
Looms but the Horror of the shade,
And yet the menace of the years
Finds, and shall find, me unafraid.

It matters not how strait the gate,
How charged with punishments the scroll.
I am the master of my fate:
I am the captain of my soul.

If you are unable to see light at the end of the tunnel, you may just be walking with your eyes closed. And if you do see light at the end of the tunnel, just make sure it is not an oncoming train.

Chaos, circumstances, obstacles may be external, but conflict is always internal. Ponder over this statement for a few minutes and you will know exactly what I mean. When you know how to resolve your internal conflict, external factors bother you less and less. In short, be mindful of your actions and reactions, work on self-purification and learn to listen to yourself.

# KARMIC TRAIL AND PSYCHIC IMPRINTS

---

Any action you perform or any thought you pursue leaves an imprint on the mind. These imprints are the basis of emotions.

---

क्लेशमूलः कर्माशयो दृष्टादृष्टजन्मवेदनीयः ꠰ (Patanjali Yoga Sutras, 2.12)

Psychic imprints, resulting from karma, accumulated over many lives condition the mind and cause one grief.

IMAGINE A SPINNING WHEEL painted with spectral hues. Since it is spinning, its face appears an illusory white. In reality, there is no white colour on the wheel. Similarly, mind is always moving. Like the spinning wheel, it creates an illusion of reality of the material world. It makes the world look like a permanent place. However, that is not so.

In order to understand your true nature — independent and cleared of all conditioning — your mind must acquire certain stillness. To attain that stillness and examine the nature of mind, its movement must cease. It is only after such cessation you can see the real colours. Purity of discipline in your karma helps a great deal in achieving mental stability. Whatever you do with speech, actions or words leave an imprint on your mind. The objective is to help you see how all karma have a residual trail. Such residue covers and conditions your mind.

Most yogic texts demand the practitioner to follow strict karmic and moral discipline. Truly profound, if you ask me! Getting back to karma and their residue:

Karma are of three types, namely, physical, verbal and mental. Every action leaves behind an imprint. Physical actions may produce tangible residue whereas verbal and mental karma create psychic imprints. If you analyze the trail of any karma, you would be surprised to notice how it may wane but never gets destroyed completely. It is the residue of each karma that conditions you. Let me elaborate with the help of an example. As follows:

## 1. Physical  Karma – Tangible Residue

All physical actions requiring touch are physical karma. Physical karma leave behind physical residue. Let us say you have an apple. You peel and deseed it to enjoy better taste. You eat the apple leaving the skin and seeds behind. Your action of eating the fruit has resulted in the residue of apple skin and seeds. You dispose of the uneaten parts. A cow comes and gladly accepts that as food. The residue you left behind has now impacted someone else you may not even know. That apple you consumed is now in your body. It is processed by your digestive system. Two sets of residues are formed. The one that gets absorbed in your body is now traveling in your veins by way of blood and the unabsorbed portion (read residue) is let out of your physical system by way of urine and feces. Further, bacteria and other atomic entities may feed on such excreta.

Your physical karma of eating an apple has left an imprint on you and other life-forms. The residue from the apple that is in your blood directly affects your physical health. The residue eaten by the cow has a bearing on its health and on the quality of milk it produces. The excrements from your body have an impact on atomic life-forms as well as the environment. It does not seem much, does it? Now imagine six billion humans on the planet doing that. Further, envision billions of other living creatures in the equation. The physical world is a residue of collective karma. It is the residue that matters. Your physical karma has a telling impact on you and your immediate surroundings; plus, it has an impact on the whole world. On the path to self-transformation, self-control starts by following the discipline of living.

## 2. Verbal Karma – Psychic Residue

Whether an instruction, statement, question, whatever it may be — anything you utter is verbal karma. All verbal karma leave behind psychic residue. Words uttered by you have a great impact on your mind and consciousness, as well as on the mind of those at the receiving end. A conditioned mind is supported and driven by psychic imprints. It is relatively easy to clean up physical residue, but psychic one takes much greater effort. Let's go back to the example of the apple. Further assume you are a person of fine taste and that this time you have company while eating.

The apple is deliciously fresh and crunchy, with perfect sweetness. You remark about its taste and how you have never had such an amazing apple. A few weeks later, you may not recall the taste of the apple, but you are likely to remember what you had said at the time of eating it. In fact, anytime anyone else is going to make a similar remark about other fruits, it may remind you of the apple. And here is the interesting point: if you had not uttered anything while eating that apple, it would be much easier for you to forget about the apple. Why? Because you left no psychic imprint beyond the taste and sight of the fruit. On the path of self-transformation, at some point in time, one ought to observe strict verbal discipline.

## 3. Mental Karma – Psychic Imprint

The subtlest and the most powerful of the three karmas is mental karma. It leaves behind a permanent trail; an imprint that is hard to erase. The origin of karma of any type is a thought. Pursuit of a thought is mental karma. It has an immediate impact on your mental state, a lasting impact on your consciousness and an everlasting effect, however subtle, on your mind. Once again, let's go back to our example of eating an apple. This time, you don't have the apple with you. The thought of an apple crosses your mind. You don't drop that thought. Instead, you start to pursue it. From the original thought of the apple, you are reminded of the time you last had an apple. That thought may link you to the thought of buying the apple from the shop.

Just note that the initial apple-thought has now shifted and you are now thinking about the shop. The shop owner's picture and communication flashes in front of you. You recall giving money to the seller. You remember another customer, who was buying bananas, standing next to you. You further recall how she was carefully picking the bananas and her physical attributes. You are now reminded of her statements, her voice and how she paid the shopkeeper. You are tossed back to the thought of the shopkeeper because he returned your change with your bag of apples. You take the bag and start walking. You are now reminded of the market conditions. You may further recall some unpleasant incident that happened one time in the market. And on and on and on...

Had you dropped the thought of apple at the very moment it emerged, you would not have gone through the grind of mental karma. And all this depends on your memory. Only if you had remembered to not think of things other than the object of your meditation, you would have enjoyed a lucid, crisp and gratifying session of meditation. I hope you know that an average human being goes through sixty-thousand thoughts during the course of twenty-four hours. No wonder you enjoy sleep! At least, you get some break. The act of concentration is designed to instill a discipline of mental karma. And, the art of meditation is to maintain that state.

Memory has a very important role to play in correct meditation. When you are able to retain only a part of your memory, that is — the object of meditation, you are moving towards achieving the tranquil state. However, memory is also your greatest hurdle in meditating correctly. Primarily because your memory is an accumulation, a storage tank, of your psychic imprints.

अनुभूतविषयासंप्रमोषः स्मृतिः | (Patanjali Yoga Sutras, 1.11)

A function of consciousness, memory is the unaltered collection of words and experiences.

It's not possible to empty your memory store. However, it's possible to drop the thought as soon as it starts to emerge.

That leads to a state of non-recollection. When you hold your mind in the tranquil absorptive state, afflictions from psychic imprints start to fade.

Your mind operates on the famous computing principle of GIGO — Garbage In, Garbage Out. If you do ill, speak ill and think ill, the residue is going to leave you sick. If you do well, speak well and think well, the outcome is going to be well. Excess of anything results in excess residue. The more you eat, the greater the inventory, the bigger the headache of managing it. Imagine having a warehouse stocked up with unnecessary widgets. Your mind is a warehouse. Don't stock it up with useless stuff. Watch what you do, say and think; transformation will begin automatically.

The supreme yogi, Krishna says to Arjuna:

यथा दीपो निवातस्थो नेङ्गते सोपमा स्मृता ।
योगिनो यतचित्तस्य युञ्जतो योगमात्मनः ॥ (Bhagavad Gita 6.19)

The conquered mind of the yogi is still like the unflickering lamp in a place devoid of wind.

In the absence of wind, the flame stays steady; similarly, a tranquil mind remains still in the absence of desires. And once again: desires are simply thoughts that you haven't been able to drop. With an ever present mind that has turned inward or surrendered to the Divine, you will never find yourself pursuing unwanted thoughts. In that state of non-pursuit, how can there be any disagreeable reactions from you? In the light of the vigilance of the still mind, how can there be any deviation from the object of your meditation (read bliss)? A mind that has gone empty fills with love naturally.

Just like your body gets tired after prolonged physical

work; just like you get tired if you speak continuously for long periods, your mind gets tired from unceasing mental karma. A complete adoption of the yoga of self-transformation in your life, living and character will allow you to enjoy deep dives into the ocean of bliss within you. A fit body, restrained speech and a calm mind — the natural outcome of correctly treading the path.

# MIND AND IMPURE THOUGHTS

Mind is like a monkey, forever hopping from one place to another. It's not pure-impure or good-bad. It just is.

"IS IT A SIN to have impure thoughts? How can I get rid of such thoughts?" someone wrote to me the other day. Before I answer this question, allow me to share with you that I don't believe in the notion of sin. There's nothing called sin. I'm not suggesting that everything we do or think is right, but sin means you have done something that has led to estrangement from God, because of which God is now upset with you. I don't think God would be God if He got upset. God's love is unconditional. Sin is a religious concept, whereas your true nature and God, too, is beyond any religion, book or belief system.

If there's no sin, does that mean everything is acceptable? Not quite. Nature operates on a self-fulfilling prophecy. You plant an apple seed and it'll sprout and grow into an apple tree. Nature is not punishing you or rewarding you for this karma. To judge as good or bad/right or wrong is the human way. The divine way is to simply be aware, to be a witness. There is no sin in having impure thoughts, but acting on impure thoughts can amount to undesirable actions. And, this leads me to the topic of how to rise above your impure thoughts?

If anyone ever tells you that they can give you a practice, or a way to not have impure thoughts, they are lying. No power in this world or any other can give you that guarantee. As I mentioned earlier, an average human mind goes through sixty-thousand thoughts in twenty-four hours, and, it is but natural that some of those thoughts are going to be undesirable. To have an impure thought doesn't make you impure; it doesn't make you a bad person.

It's not the thought itself that matters, it's what you do with it.

Everyone experiences thoughts of hatred, jealousy and impropriety. There's nothing destructive about it, because a thought can come from any direction, at any time. One could be thinking about philandering or deceiving someone while praying in a temple and the same person could be thinking of compassion and morality in a brothel. It's possible. Thoughts are involuntary, they come uninvited. There's nothing unusual about having impure thoughts. It's not the thought itself but its pursuit that ultimately impacts your emotional and mental state.

Therefore, it's not realistic to expect that you never have any impure thoughts but it's quite doable to not pursue such thoughts or act on them. When you get a thought you deem impure, simply shift your attention. Focus your mind elsewhere. Don't go after the thought. Let's say you are thanking God for everything you have in your life, including a wonderful family. And, out of nowhere, the thought of a woman surfaces in your consciousness. At that moment, don't chase the thought or feel bad that you thought what you did. Just gently bring your attention back to the present moment, the woman will go away.

If, however, you start to follow the thought-trail and begin contemplating on her, her body, or being with her, the thought will rapidly gather momentum, soon overpowering your ability to think straight. A tiny, harmless flake of snow will turn into a juggernaut as it rolls down. It may nudge you to translate your thought into an action you may regret later on.

A disciple fell in love with her master. She felt guilty for feeling those emotions, but guilt could not help her emerge stronger than her ardor. With her heart ruling over her mind, she could contain it no longer.

"I'm sorry, master," she said, "but, I have tremendous feelings for you."

"Don't be sorry," said the master. "If you have tremendous feelings for me, I've enough discipline for both of us."

Think of yourself as the master and your thoughts as the disciple. When they come to you, no one has to be sorry, you just have to be aware and choose a course of action accordingly. Give your thoughts the freedom to approach you, while you keep the strength to direct them. If you repeatedly get the same impure thought, then, we need to get to the bottom of it. It could be because of deprivation. Those who are fulfilled in their lives are lot less likely to experience constant jealousy or hatred than those who never experienced true love.

If someone's fasting, it's quite natural that they'll get thoughts of food more than anybody else. So long as they are busy, they may not feel hungry, but the moment they're free, the thought of food will emerge strongly. Similarly, when you give your mind a free moment, most probably you'll have an impure thought, a negative thought or a depressing thought. It's natural. Why? Because, most people are constantly battling with themselves to not think impurely, not to be negative, not to be jealous and so forth.

Mindfulness is the key. Accept, don't react, don't pursue, don't feel guilty. Just let it be. You can build mindfulness with meditation, with contemplation, with determination. You never have to be sorry for your feelings or your thoughts. They are not pure or impure, they just are. You just have to watch out what you do with them.

When you simply draw yourself back to the present moment, all thoughts, both good and bad, vanish. There's no battle then. There's nothing to escape in the present moment. This is the simple truth.

# A Beautiful Life

What if there was no death and we were immortal?
Would life be better if it was eternal?

ONE AFTERNOON I RETURNED to my hut after meeting ashram visitors; it had just stopped raining. Almost. It was drizzling lightly giving the feeling as if you were standing in the misty clouds. Soon that stopped, too. I could hear birds chirping at a distance.

The winter sun playfully peeked out of the clouds spreading the blanket of warm light on my study table. The tweeting of the birds felt closer. I got up and looked outside the window. Oh, what a beauty! Tens of little sparrows were merrily scuttling about pecking the ground in search of food. Their movements were synchronized. I watched the divine rhythm for a good few minutes. The sky became gray and it was raining again. The sparrows went quiet and then disappeared like rainbow in a blue sky.

Mountains stood where they were and the river continued to flow indifferently. Everything in the world was going on as it had been earlier. I was awestruck. There was something so simple about those beautiful little birds, their act, which made me almost slip into deep *samadhi*. They came out when the sun emerged, got to work, and went away in hiding when it rained. Simple.

Simplicity is spirituality.

Even meditation is done so that you understand yourself better, so you may examine your life with discerning wisdom and delayer yourself. Correct meditation leads to expansion of consciousness, which makes you childlike. You begin to see things and phenomena without judgments. You realize that any complexity in your life is merely your interpretation of how you see or experience anything. A sense of simplicity helps you to declutter your physical and mental space.

When your headspace is clear, your life becomes simple automatically. You naturally develop a spiritual outlook. And how to know if you are inching towards spirituality? For one thing, you start to see everything as a blessing in life. The temporary and transient nature of this world bothers you no longer. As you delve deeper into your own infinite existence, you become increasingly unafraid. Because at the root of this spirituality is the simple understanding — everything is a blessing.

There was a yogi who manifested God with his searing penance and asked for the boon of immortality. God made him immortal and the yogi was filled with pride. He settled down in a village and began harassing the villagers by forcing them to serve him at his beck and call. Knowing that he was immortal, the villagers submitted to his demands, but his atrocities only increased.

In the same village lived a burly wrestler, who decided enough was enough.

"I'll break every bone in your body and pull your eyeballs out," he said to the immortal yogi.

"Ha! No one can kill me."

The wrestler pounced on the yogi and surely enough, crushed every bone in his body and left him blind. With the boon of imperishability, however, he wouldn't die. But at the same time, with a body that could no longer move, eyes that could not see anymore, he lost all desire to live. People took their revenge on him and he was left alone to die. But die he could not.

Eventually, he figured that death was the only way to end his suffering. He fervently prayed for death. All he wanted to do was die. He realized that immortality wasn't a boon. At least, death would give him a chance to be born again and not make the same mistakes. He would get a new body, a new lease of life, he thought.

I'm not saying that anyone should pray for death or close out the account of their life. I'm simply saying that most of us want to hold onto eternity, a sort of permanence. The truth is when you see life not as a burden but boon, when you see its temporary nature not as a shortcoming but solution, life feels like a big blessing then.

Since we are here, we may as well live with gratitude and positivity. We are already at the party; we may as well rejoice and join in the festivities. What's the point in sitting in a corner brooding and whining? It's not going to lift anyone's mood (including yours). We may as well celebrate life, celebrate you.

The parents of a child were distressed when they lost Tinker, their pet dog. They didn't know how to explain death to their five-year-old son.

"What happened to Tinker, mummy? Why isn't he moving?"

"He's dead, sonny," the mother replied.

"He's gone to heaven, to be with God."

"Why?" the child said innocently. "What's God gonna do with a dead dog?"

If we are not frolicking with life while we are here, if we are not sportive while we have a chance, how could we possibly enjoy anything in any other world (or lifetime)? After all, we carry the same tendencies forward. It's now or never. This is it, this life, however it is, it's a boon. Why live it any other way?

Sparrows come when the sun is out; they hunt for food and fly back to their nests in the evening. Quite similarly, the soul finds a womb when the time is right, lives a life and goes back to merge with the Supreme Consciousness. Or, it is reborn to fulfill its desires, like the hungry bird that continues flying in search of food. This is the cycle of samsara. This is the mystical play of nature. Transient but eternal. Sophisticated yet simple.

At any rate, it is a blessing. Like our lives, like our planet. Beautiful.

# LOVE

# WHEN CARE DESTROYS LOVE

---

Obsessive care cripples love just like excessive water
destroys plants.

---

HAVE YOU EVER DREADED approaching your partner to talk
about even something as simple as what you wish to do over
the weekend? And then played the conversation in your
head over and over again before speaking to her (or him)?
Only because you don't know how she would react. Or more
importantly, you fear that your partner would respond most
unfavorably, get mad at you or even throw tantrums.

If you have, then you must be familiar with that churning
feeling in your stomach —that obnoxious hollowness in your
tummy, that sinking feeling as if you are on the roller-coaster,
going down at breakneck speed. You can hear your heartbeat
loud and clear, you suddenly feel low. Then, you slip into
excessive worrying. How will she take it this time? How will
you cope with her reaction? So on and so forth. You tremble
at the thought of broaching the topic.

And then you wait and wait. You wait for that "perfect
moment" to talk to her. You hope that she would listen to

you this time, so you may really speak your heart out without worrying about her reaction. You keep playing the tape in your head because you want to be careful with your words, you love her and you don't want to hurt her, but you also want to voice your feelings. You prepare yourself mentally for the outburst, but nothing prepares you, really. They don't react any differently. You walk away feeling the same as always — unheard, guilty, low and hurt.

If you know what I mean, then let me tell you that you need help. But it's your partner who's emotionally troubled or obsessed, you say. Of course. Even then, *you* need help.

You have taken upon yourself the unrealistic job of managing the feelings of the other person. Rather than making them understand that they are responsible for their conduct and emotions, you have burdened yourself by thinking that your actions can fix your partner's feelings. Big mistake.

In a healthy relationship, two people are there for each other but they take care of themselves, too. The partners understand that they must take responsibility for their own lives. When this responsibility shifts to just one partner, such a relationship is doomed. It's neither sustainable nor practical. It's not even right, if you ask me.

Here's a simple but profound story that has been doing the rounds on the internet. I first read it in self-help author Melody Beattie's *Codependent No More*.

A woman moved to a cave in the mountains to study with a guru. In her quest of knowledge, she wanted to learn everything there was to learn, she said. The guru gave her stacks of books and left her alone, so she could study.

"Have you learned everything there is to know yet?" he would ask her every morning.

"No," she would say every time, "I haven't."

The guru would then strike her over the head with a cane. This went on for months. Same question, same answer, same treatment. One morning, however, when he raised his cane to hit her, the woman grabbed the cane from the guru, stopping the assault in midair.

Relieved to end the daily beatings, but fearing reprisal, the woman looked up at her guru. To her surprise, the guru smiled.

"Congratulations," he said, "you have graduated. You now know everything there is to know."

"How come?" asked the woman.

"You have learned that you will never learn everything there is to know," he replied, "and you have learned how to stop the pain."

Your pain stops the moment you realize that you can't possibly cover all the scenarios in a relationship, that you can't correct the feelings and thoughts of the other person, that they, too, must take some (if not complete) responsibility for their own lives. You learn to watch out for yourself. It's not that you love the other person any less now; in fact, your love increases because the toxicity is replaced by responsibility.

In a toxic relationship, there's a serious lack of understanding about what the other person wants. Obsessed partners are expert controllers; not necessarily manipulators, but controllers. They can extract a certain behavior from you by exhibiting their excessive reliance on you. They are not doing so consciously or cunningly. They are only acting compulsively, often based on what has worked for them till date. Soon, however, it gets suffocating for both people because it's tiring and taxing. There's little room left to play as any space is overtaken by worry and fear. So, what is the solution, you ask?

An excited woman called her husband from work.

"Guess what!" she screamed with joy, "I just won the jackpot! I'm richer by $20 million!"

"You're kidding me!" the husband yelled, equally ecstatic.

"Pack your clothes," she said, "Oh! I could do with a break!"

"Winter or summer clothes?"

"All of them. I want you out of the house by six."

Detachment is your answer. I'm not saying that you do it like the woman in the anecdote. And, I don't mean it in some cryptic theological or philosophical sense.

Here's how I see detachment in the context of relationships. Physical distance is not detachment (although it can help sometimes). Detachment is giving the other person time and space, so they may learn to be more responsible. It is a reminder that you can't take care of the other person without taking care of yourself first. It is the understanding that you, too, deserve to do things that make you happy. You've as much right to life as anyone else.

Detachment is an acknowledgement of the fact that the people you love are responsible for their feelings. By letting them take control of their (and not your) life, you are actually helping them. It may hurt initially, but eventually, it infuses a new vitality in your relationship. It's about developing a sort of neutrality, so you don't start worrying about little things and feel the urge to fix everything right away. You can't fix what you didn't create. Not all the time, anyway.

Detachment is the realization that most troubled partners don't act badly as a matter of choice. Their coping mechanisms propel them to behave a certain way. But your sense of detachment will give you the peace required to handle everything far more effectively (without going crazy). Detachment is taking it easy (not for granted) in the face of friction and conflict. It is about examining your reaction rather than acting on the first thought or the first feeling you experience when things go haywire. Detachment helps you to keep your sanity until your partner understands that neither of you can always be on your toes.

If you wish to have a healthy relationship, sooner or later you'll have to stand up for yourself. True love naturally has a degree of detachment otherwise it becomes too clingy and uncomfortable. People in unhealthy relationships are prisoners of obsession and attachment. Healthy relationships, on the other hand, are fueled by friendship and freedom. Obsessive care undermines love.

Learn to speak up for yourself. Don't be scared. Breathe. Detach. Make no attempt to fix everything this instant. No one is going to die if you start caring about yourself. On the contrary, your life and others' too will only become more beautiful if you stand your ground and find your feet, because, ultimately, this new-found strength will make you even more loving, caring, confident and happy.

# THE DRAMA TRIANGLE

---

Love flows without resentment, like water from a
mountain, in the one who learns to love himself first.

---

IN THE PREVIOUS CHAPTER, I cited a popular story from Melody
Beattie's *Codependent No More*. Continuing my thoughts on
the subject of relationships, I would like to begin by quoting
a passage from the same book.

Sometimes, my youngest son, Shane, hangs on too tightly
and too long after a hug. He starts tipping me over. I lose
my balance, and become impatient for him to stop hugging
me. I begin to resist him. Perhaps he does it to keep me
close to him a little longer. Maybe it's a form of control over
me. I don't know. One night when he did this my daughter
watched until even she became frustrated and impatient.

"Shane," she said, "there comes a time to let go."

For each of us, there comes a time to let go. You will
know when that time has come. When you have done all
that you can do, it is time to detach. Deal with your feelings.
Face your fears about losing control. Gain control of yourself

and your responsibilities. Free others to be who they are. In doing so, you will set yourself free.


Personally, this instruction makes great sense to me. By detachment, I don't mean that you break up with your partner. Though, I agree that sometimes there's no other choice. Presently, however, my focus is building a sense of detachment while you are still in the relationship. If you cling too hard for too long, you both will eventually tip over.

When you continue to ignore yourself, you may provide what your partner is looking for, but ultimately, neither of you will be happy. It does more damage than good to the relationship. If you are the one who always has to act strong and be the provider, one day it'll break you completely. This leads me to my point of elucidation today — compulsive care.

Excessive clinginess (lack of awareness of personal space in a relationship) and/or undue fear (not being able to voice your feelings because the other person either reacts violently or ignores what you have to say) are the classic signs of a toxic relationship. When you feel forced to care, not because you are in responsible relationship, but out of fear or attachment, you are a victim of compulsive care. And in such circumstances, you go through three emotions. It's a cycle.

By the way, my views on the current matter are neither original nor radical. Instead, what I am sharing here was first mentioned by Aristotle and later more eloquently and appositely by Dr. Stephen Karpman in his seminal work on transactional analysis. I'm merely stating my interpretation based on my own experience and observation. The three emotions, or more appropriately, the three roles, form what's called the Karpman Drama Triangle. Here:

## 1. The Rescuer

In an unbalanced relationship, one person is always playing the role of a rescuer. As a rescuer, you act strong, together, in charge. As soon as your partner plays victim and cries for help, you make yourself available for her. "Let me help you," the rescuer says. "Don't worry, I'm here." You put aside your own preferences, needs, issues and anxieties. You rise to the occasion and help your partner who is emotionally dependent on you. Sometimes, unfortunately, all a rescuer is doing is disguising his or her own issues in the name of care or compassion. They feel compulsive to be nice, to be there for the other person, at the expense of their own well-being. It comes at a great personal cost though, because once the issue is resolved, the rescuer moves to the second point in the triangle.

## 2. The Persecutor

Since the inner happiness of the rescuer disappears as soon as the matter is resolved, their own issues rise to the surface. They no longer feel that the weaker partner actually needed help. Instead, a rescuer becomes a tormentor, a sort of a persecutor. "It's all your fault," that's the first feeling he experiences towards the other person. A resentment builds up in the one who's been acting strong. The rescuer feels angry, hurt, used, even abused. This creates the desire to control the behavior of the other person, to snub them, curb them, so that such a situation does not arise again. The rescuer feels, "I must tell her that it can't go on like this." But, since the rescuer has not learned to take care of himself, and because there exists a communication gap between the two partners, he's unable to express freely. Consequently, a rescuer starts to behave like a persecutor holding the other person responsible for everything she's feeling. This does not end here though. Once, he's acted strong and then blamed the partner, he moves to the third point on the triangle.

## 3. The Victim

The rescuer now sees himself as a victim. A sense of self-pity emerges in consciousness. The person who was once a rescuer now feels helpless, powerless, indecisive and depressed. The desire to enjoy life takes a back seat and negative emotions engulf the victim. "Poor me" is the core feeling. The victim feels sorry for himself and believes that he needs someone to help them. And here's the tragic thing: a victim seeks a rescuer (or even a persecutor, because they come across strong). This's the reason why most people move from one abusive relationship to another. They keep attracting the same type of partners. Every time they think that this relationship is going to be different, it ends up the same — more or less.

It needn't be this way. It all starts with leading a responsible life. A life where you understand that in order to love someone, you must fill yourself with love first. To care for someone requires that you care about yourself first; an understanding that there's only so much you can do for the other person. That, one day, they ought to take responsibility for their behavior.

If you keep on acting strong when you are actually tired within, one day you'll fall apart. Beyond repair. Happiness maybe an individual journey, but it's a mutual feeling. If you are consistently going to be the rescuer, your partner will mostly play a victim. And, if you see yourself as a victim, you'll attract a persecutor. Either way, it's detrimental to your self-esteem and well-being.

A 25-year-old son, intending to marry his girlfriend, asked his father, "Dad, how much does a wedding cost?" "No idea, son," the father replied. "I'm still paying for it."

A relationship will be a constant burden and never a reward, unless it offers mutual fulfillment, personal space and room for exploration and expression. Yes, you should care and you should love, but it must start with yourself. Most of the life's problems disappear if you take care of yourself and treat yourself with love. If you extend yourself the same courtesy as you do to your loved ones (or even strangers), your life will take on a whole new dimension.

Neither a rescuer, nor a persecutor or a victim, the person who learns the art of self-care and self-love becomes Buddha, he becomes divine. Altruism arises naturally in those who lead fulfilling lives. And your fulfillment can't be separate from your pursuits and preferences.

No waterfalls emanate from dry mountains. They come from the ones that once absorbed rainwater, they gush forth from the ones that are full. The more love you pour in you, the more flows out of you. Fill yourself with what you wish to give out, for what's inside is what manifests outside.

# ARE YOU COMFORTABLE WITH YOURSELF?

---

A leaf, once disconnected from the source, starts to dry and decay rapidly. Stay connected for infinite joy and bliss.

---

LIVING IN THIS WORLD, most things are like clockwork. People are born, they grow up, get an education, get a job, get married, have kids, look after them and themselves, get old and pass away.

Have you ever wondered why most of us enjoy going out, watching movies, listening to music and socializing? Why do many enjoy being a part of big gatherings, crowds and go to concerts, etcetera? Society and evolution has conditioned most to seek their joy outside. Such external pursuit of happiness increases the distance, widens the gap, between who you really are and what you are projecting to be.

So, should one not pursue opportunities in the material world, or should one simply ignore their responsibilities? Not at all. On the contrary, I suggest there is nothing wrong in living the life of your dreams, especially if it involves helping others, but, my focus today is to help you gain a new perspective on many acts we consider natural and necessary.

If you spend time analyzing, you will find that all external acts make you forget about yourself. You no longer have to deal with yourself, the need to work on yourself disappears. While at the cinema, when watching TV, at a party, at a social event, amidst a gathering, you are connecting with an external source; you move away from who you are, the environment around you molds your mental state, it gains control of you, it disconnects you from the source.

The other day, outside my hut, a green tree was swaying wild in the gusty winds, its leaves fluttering rapidly, as if playing. The sky was cloudy, the river was choppy, mountains were lush green and at a distance I could see cattle grazing. A great deal of activity was going on in the nature but it was still utterly peaceful and serene. I turned my attention back on the leaves. They were dancing; they were swinging in frenzy, as if trying to detach themselves from the tree, seeking greater freedom outside, as if they knew that once detached they would fly far and high in the mighty wind.

Just then a leaf managed to shake loose; it was not with the tree anymore; it flew tens of feet high in the air before crash-landing in a puddle. *The leaf that was green earlier would start to rot soon*, I thought. Even though it gained freedom, because it got disconnected from its source, it lost its ability to derive nourishment and strength. It lay there lifeless. When the leaf was united with the tree, it was able to get nutrition from water and earth. Now, even though both the elements were still there in the puddle, they will no longer nurture the leaf, only decay it.

No matter what you do in the world, feel free to enjoy, be yourself, but do not uncouple yourself from the source, the Divine, the primordial energy, the quintessential seed you have sprouted from. Any freedom you gain by disengaging from the source is short-lived and temporary.

How to find out if you are still connected to the root? Going to shrines or chanting the holy names are no indicators. They are mere activities, external activities in fact. The greatest sign that you are one with the source is when you are comfortable in your own company, at peace within; it means you have mostly turned inwards; you have understood and absorbed the essence of spirituality.

Once upon a time, a king, accompanied by his retinue, approached a sage in his cave in the deep Himalayan woods. It had a small entrance.

The king bent down and entered the cave. There was pin drop silence inside.

"Oh, you must feel very lonely here, Master." the king said. "Now that you are here, I am lonely indeed," the sage said, "earlier I was so enjoying my company. You are in touch with others, you are connected to them, so you feel lonely when they are not around, whereas I am in touch with myself and I feel lonely when I am not around."

If you wish to find out how comfortable you are with yourself, in your own company, practice solitude for a few days and analyze yourself. You will begin to understand what I mean. Once again, I am not suggesting that you stop enjoying in the material world. In fact, when you are connected to the source, when you are comfortable with yourself, any joy you get from any activity grows multifold, it gets magnified, you experience happiness and bliss like never before.

When you enjoy being with yourself, the whole world will find joy and peace in your company. The more at ease you are with yourself, the greater your inner peace remains unaffected by what goes on around you. Like a leaf on a tree, when you remain connected to the source, you dance when it is windy, you gain nutrition from mud and water. Once uncoupled though, the same wind will toss you around, earth will decompose you, the same water that irrigated the tree once will disintegrate the leaf.

What you have inside is infinitely more important than what you don't have outside, what you have within gives you the perspective to see all that is without.

# SINGLE PARENTS AND BROKEN MARRIAGES

---

Give yourself a chance to bloom and say no to an abusive marriage. Never allow anyone to crush your dignity.

---

LAST MONTH A FEW readers emailed me separately about a similar issue: disharmony in relationships. I decided to club their comments.

"I've been married for 15 years and have done everything I could but my husband still gets mad like hell. He swears at me and shouts as if I am an unwanted servant in the house. It all happens over tiny matters and this is his general behavior towards me. I have left him so many times, but went back to him because every time he promised not to repeat his behavior...

"I thought of a divorce but didn't go for it for the sake of my children because I believe that children from single families become more timid, moody and have psychological issues. What to do when it just doesn't work with your partner?"

While I'm not a psychologist, trained or otherwise, I can shed some light from a spiritual perspective. First of all, there's no clear evidence to suggest that children brought up by single parents turn out any less in any way compared to those with both parents. Some of the kindest and most adorable people I've known were raised by single parents.

There is no doubt that children in single families miss the presence of the other parent, there is no conclusive proof either that this void has far-reaching psychological or other implications. On the contrary, children of single parents tend to take their own relationships more seriously because they have already experienced the fragility of it.

What matters more is not whether a child has been raised by a single parent, but whether she's been provided a loving environment, conducive to personal growth. And, this is really the spiritual perspective I wish to offer: a close-knit family with fewer people is infinitely better than a toxic one with more people. When two partners frequently argue, quarrel and fight, this has a telling impact on the child. In such a case, in my opinion, it's better to split and be at peace, than live in a tense, unpredictable and unhealthy environment. An abuser must be shunned.

Going back to my readers' questions: the decision of separation is never an easy one. No, not because you don't know right from wrong, but because in most abusive relationships, the dominating partner is often unpredictable and inconsistent. You don't know what will tick them off. They can be very loving one moment and an absolute monster the next. This is torturous and intimidating for the family members. And this sort of environment is far more damaging than being raised by a single parent.

Inconsistency in the behavior of the other person is what makes most relationships particularly complicated. What's even worse is that an abusive partner rarely changes his or her ways. When they are fickle and discordant, they'll remain like that with you. I also want to make an important point here: don't think that it's in their nature to be angry. They are — albeit not necessarily consciously — choosing to be this way with you because you've accepted their misbehavior in the past.

Most abusive partners come across as loving and respectful at the beginning of a new relationship, but, as time goes by, they become increasingly condescending, even manipulative. If you keep on accepting their misdemeanor, they'll continue to misbehave. Never for the sake of a child or for any other reason should you ever put up with a partner who mistreats you. They treated you well when they were courting you, didn't they? It means that they are capable of good behavior and now you are being taken for granted. If you are financially independent, move on. If you are not, seek financial independence as a matter of priority.

If you don't move out of an abusive relationship, you are doing yourself great disservice. If you just can't call it quits, then you must develop your personal method to keep your sanity. Whether your coping mechanism is compassion or shopping, forgiveness or meditation, it's your personal choice. Some have more peculiar methods though:

"What do you do when your husband shouts at you?" A woman asked her friend.

"I start cleaning," her friend replied.

"Cleaning?" She was surprised.

"You don't shout back or get mad?"

"Nope. I simply clean the washroom."

"Never heard this one before! It won't work for me for sure."

"Well, when I clean the toilet bowl with his toothbrush, it gives me immense satisfaction."

Hopefully, you have a more hygienic approach. Humor aside, if you are going to treat yourself second-rate by accepting or ignoring offensive behavior, please know that you'll have to face it till your last breath. Your partner won't improve or change. Better than getting caught up in social definitions of right and wrong is to lead a life of peace and respect.

A life of dignity is your birthright. Don't discount it.

# Afraid Of Getting Old

---

You are old when your memories are no longer bridges
but boulders that obstruct your present journey.

---

ARE YOU AFRAID OF getting old? All those who see death at a ripe age have to go through old age. There are some who keep defying it till their last breath and there are many who start feeling old even in their forties. Does human body become more fragile as people age? Well, general observation of the world around us certainly vouches for that. But what if, hypothetically speaking, we removed one's physical age from the equation? The concept of old age will get a new definition perhaps. I have known numerous people who lived through abusive relationships, who suffered torment, trauma and torture for the most part of their life only so they could have someone around when they get old. The fear of being alone when old can really haunt some. So, when does one get old? Read on.

When your life has more memories than ambition, consider yourself old. When all you have to talk about is how you did this in the past or how you did that in the past, how you were amazing a decade ago or how you were so incredible back then. When you no longer live in your present or look up to your future, when all you do is reknit the same stories in the present using yarn of the past, you are old. An unfailing sign of the one who feels old within is they mostly talk about their past.

Old age is inevitable for all blessed with a normal lifespan. When anything is inevitable, it means you only have two choices: first, handle it with grace and gratitude or second, deny it with griping and whining. Old age is like the Friday afternoon at work — it gets quiet, it slows down before the weekend break. And what is death? Well, death is the weekend. Consciousness moves on. If you believe in soul or rebirth, a new birth awaits you. If you believe in heaven or hell, who knows, you may just live a life of your dreams in one of those places. If you don't believe in anything, well then, hopefully you know your own answer.

A priest went to a rich man's funeral. The deceased was his friend and a hardcore atheist, who vehemently refuted any notion of God, heaven or hell. It was an elaborate funeral. He approached the coffin. It was made from exquisite teakwood, soft satin lining inside, the body was clad in handcrafted silk robe. "Oh what a shame," exclaimed the priest, "all dressed up and nowhere to go!"

Personally, if you ask me, I am at perfect ease with any of your belief. Whatever gives you inner strength and gives you a sense of peace, adopt that belief. After all, these all are theories anyway — some more convincing than the others. That's all. They are not capable of manifesting the truth for you. At the most, they give you an intellectual choice, a way of living.

The quality of your breath, the basis of your life, does not deteriorate till the last moment. So, you may as well enjoy the various seasons of life. What others think of you is their problem. Deep within, you know yourself better than anyone else. The world or the society will try their best to make you feel old. Why, even parents, elders, teachers keep telling you to grow up or that you are grown up now. They are not doing it intentionally, they just don't know any better. Often. Have no grudges against them, just learn to increase the volume of your inner voice. It will guide you and help you decide your course of action.

One day, when Mulla Nasruddin of age ninety decided to marry a girl who was only eighteen, his sons, grandchildren and great grandchildren were appalled.

"What are you doing, father?" the son said, "Fatima's only eighteen!"

"So what? Even your mother was eighteen when I first married her."

"You don't get it, do you? Let me be straight up with you; copulation at this age? It may result in someone's death! I'm warning you."

"Aah...don't get all worked up like your mother used to, you stress-head! Don't worry, if Fatima dies, I'll marry another one!" Mulla said.

I am not saying you kill reason and sense; just don't let anyone ever dictate the way you feel about yourself — no teacher, no preacher, no religion, no authority, no partner. The legal system, your faith and those around you may give you a framework of living, but you alone should set your rules of life. When distant memories become obstacles in covering the distance of your present journey, take charge of your life, your present, and start living! With compassion for others and yourself, make the most of every moment.

Childhood does not last forever. Youth is not permanent, and old age will end too. Nothing is worth clinging onto. These are fleeting seasons. Live, love, laugh, give while you have. Do so in such a manner that you fall in love with the person you see in the mirror, in a way so there is no burden on your conscience when you put your head down on the pillow.

What I longed for will be set aside
The things I pursued in vain —
Let them pass
Let me turn
To things I overlooked
And carelessly threw away
To possess them truly until they are mine.

(Rabindranath Tagore, The Stars Look On)

Be yourself. Love yourself. Know yourself. You will find yourself beyond age.

# Handling Criticism

---

What they see in you is a reflection of their very self.
What you don't have in you, you can't see in others.

---

CRITICISM IS INEVITABLE. IT is always an opinion of the other person. If you agree with other people's judgment, their criticism may prompt you to improve yourself. However, if you disagree, you may be embracing negativity. Negative emotions weaken you. Sometimes, it can be hard to deal with criticism, especially if it comes from your loved ones. When others try to unload their negativity and opinions onto you, at that moment, you have a choice, an option to reject, to discard, to let go. If you can let go, you will remain peaceful; your heart will not be wounded, certainly not as much. Let me share a story with you:

There was a certain monastery in Japan. It was founded by a Chinese master long time ago. The master and his followers were known for destroying religious texts and other such artifacts like Buddha's statues and religious symbols. Their rationale was to free themselves from any form of conditioning and attachment. They believed that such symbols and texts conditioned and shackled the mind, rather than freeing it. Radical methods of the Chinese masters helped many gain the transcendental state. However, those who disagreed with their methods criticized them heavily.

Once, two seekers, well-educated, one even a professor from North America, visited that monastery. They were fairly well-read and had preconceived notions about the place and its founder. The abbot received them and took them around for a tour of the monastery. Towards the end of the tour, the *Roshi*, elder master, led them into a ceremonial hall to pay respects to a statue of the founder by prostrating and offering incense.

The two seekers were disturbed as they had read all about the founder and his radical acts. Although disconcerted, they followed quietly.

When the *Roshi* bowed before the statue, the professor could no longer contain himself and blurted out, "This man you idolize, he burned and spat on Buddha statues! Why do you bow before him?" "If you want to spit, you spit," replied the *Roshi* calmly, "I prefer to bow."

There you go. Whether you spit or bow is your choice, and whether they bow or spit is their choice. You exercise yours and let them exercise theirs. I am reminded of a quote: "Those who love you don't need an explanation, and those who don't, are not going to believe one anyway." When you are offered criticism, you may choose to clarify your position, only if you truly wish to do that. You may wish to reflect on it, for, such criticism may even be true. Beyond that, do not cause yourself grief by brooding over others' thoughts and opinions. Reject it. Promptly.

Your freedom, inner bliss, is entirely in your own hands.

It is your own state of mind. What you do not accept can never affect you. Just like you, everyone has a right to their opinion. Till you rise above criticism, you must discover your own method to deal with it. Here are some of the popular ones for you:

1. **Remove yourself physically**: If you can remove yourself physically, you will no longer hear their opinions. If you are unable to hear what they are able to say, you will not be grieved. You may choose to go out or go for a walk.

2. **Disappear mentally**: If you can find something else to focus on, so that you are listening to your inner music, you will retain your blissful state. It is like listening to your iPod while the other person is watching TV. They are doing what they like and you are doing what you like.

3. **Visualize**: Choose a visualization that may help you. When someone decides to turn on their FM channel, you may see them as a blabbering child, a radio, or anything else that insulates you.

4. **Sympathize**: If you pay attention you will discover that those who criticize you are full of their own insecurities. Those in bliss and peace do not criticize. They may politely offer their point of view, but you will not see them criticize. Next time when you are faced with criticism, fill your heart with empathy towards the other person. They might have had a rough childhood or an unfulfilling life. This is the only way they have learned to protect and express themselves. The method of sympathizing is the most compassionate way. If you can practice this, not only will you experience great peace, you will trigger a subtle transformation in the other person, too.

Just like upon boarding a plane your destiny is in the hands of the pilot, when you take the flight of an argument, it is no longer about you alone. If you choose to react or respond to criticism in kind, you have just procreated a new entity of disharmony and negativity, you have already boarded at that time. The control is less and less in your hands. You may unnaturally curb other person's response if you exercise greater authority, but the damage is already done.

How about when you are criticizing? If you are not kind enough, big enough, to appreciate what the other person is doing for you, do not be so small to criticize either. There is a difference between helping someone improve and being downright negative about what they are doing. If you do not understand their point of view, it does not mean they are wrong. Be fair. Remember the two sets of rules?

Yes, you want to make a point. Yes, you really believe the other person is at fault. Surely, you know what all they can do to improve. There is no doubt in your mind that you are impartial and your statements, genuine. The truth is, the other person feels exactly the same about herself.

It is all in you, not all about you!

# THE ART OF APOLOGY

---

An apology is genuine when you don't repeat your
offense and when you offer no excuse.

---

FIFTEEN YEARS AGO, I was leading a large technology team at
a multi-billion dollar media company in Australia. I had just
taken over a major portfolio, and a certain issue in the new
software was affecting our users and our revenues. As the
Tech Lead, it was my responsibility to fix it. We called in
many technical experts from various firms, but no one could
pinpoint the cause. Weeks went by and we were without a
headway still. One time, pensive and introspective, I got home
an hour past midnight. I stepped into the shower and had an
epiphany. I suddenly knew how to fix the error. I couldn't wait
to get back to work and left again after a snooze.

At work, it was utterly quiet in the wee hours of the
morning. I fired up my machine, tried the fix, and voilà, it
worked. I bypassed our version control system with great
confidence, logged in as the super-user on the staging server.
(This was where we showcased our software for business
approval before rolling it out to the whole world.) I issued a

command to clean up the existing directory so I could copy across the new code. I was particularly happy imagining how amazed the executive team would be to come to work in the morning and hear this good news. Here was a simple fix that worked, where hundreds and thousands of dollars had failed.

There was a small problem, however; after I started the command on the server, I realized my faux pas. I had executed a command that was deleting everything (including the system files) from the root up.

It had effectively formatted the server. Imagine intending to merely turn the light off your room but ending up cutting the power-supply of your entire town. My act was even worse — I had burnt down the power station, too.

It took the hardware team four days to restore the server, for, apparently, there was some issue with the tape-backups, too. I was deeply embarrassed. There were many excuses to support my mistake— lack of sleep, pressure at work, ludicrous work hours, cryptic nature of the bug, deficient networking team and so forth, but they were just that, excuses. I offered none. I simply apologized to all the stakeholders. Because, the truth was, I had made an expensive mistake. Fortunately, it all ended well. Two months later, I got a substantial raise; one of the reasons they gave me was "the courage to accept, correct, and learn from the mistake."

To err is human; we all make mistakes. That, however, can't be the justification to repeat them. There are only two ways to show that we have realized our mistake: first, by not repeating it and second, by offering a sincere apology. The second point is my focus today, that is, how to apologize? Apologizing correctly is neither an art nor any craft. It is simply being natural and truthful. When we genuinely regret our action, the right words come out automatically, and seeking forgiveness becomes easier.

An apology is restoration of faith. It is conveying that 'I let you down once, but you can trust me that I won't put you through this again'. When we make a mistake, it shakes the trust of the other person. Most positive emotions rest on trust alone. For example, when you love someone, you trust them to be the way you perceive them to be or the way they project themselves. But, when they act to the contrary, it betrays your trust. This betrayal causes grief and it hurts you and it affects your love and feelings for the other person.

No apology is sincere if you plan on repeating the offense. Think of a broken pot. You can put it together once if you are careful and patient but break it again and the task is a lot more difficult now, almost impossible. Similarly, when you break someone's trust, they may forgive you once but if you do it again, you can't reasonably expect them to forget it and put it behind. Hence, an apology is meaningless if it's insincere. And what is a sincere apology, you ask?

An apology is genuine when you are determined not to repeat your offense, when you offer no excuse or justification, when you take complete responsibility of your act, and when you do so remorsefully. An apology without a sense of remorse is a pointless exercise. In fact, it's going to hurt the other person even more. Often, people say, "I'm sorry but I thought this or that...", or, "I'm sorry but the reason I did it was abc or xyz...", or, "I'm sorry if my actions hurt you." These are not apologies, but excuses.

Conjunctions like *if* and *but* have no room in a true apology. Saying why you did it is no good either. The best apology is to understand, to feel, to completely accept, and unconditionally so, that our actions have caused pain to the other person. Don't pollute your apology by citing a reason or a justification; don't ruin it by saying something without meaning it. It'll hurt the other person even more. You can either choose an apology or an excuse, not both.

A pukka apology is about coming clean and owning up to the offense.

# A WORD ON COMPASSION

---

Think of compassion as sacrifice. It is putting the other person's interests before your own. It's a choice.

---

LIFE IS LIKE THE sky, sometimes cloudy, other times very clouded. The same sky offers a completely different view depending on the time of the day. At night, it is full of stars and the waning or the waxing moon. During the day, it is full of light. Artificial lighting of cities make the beautiful star-studded sky hazy. The same sky when covered with clouds hides both the very bright sun or the soft moon. Clouds seem to come from nowhere, followed by rain. Sometimes, the same cloudy sky dislodges a hailstorm, other times, the very quiet but cold snow.

"Are you compassionate?"

"Most of the time," they answer.

"Are you forgiving?"

"Yes, most of the time," they reply.

This is the most common response to my two questions, no matter whom I ask. To tell you the truth, when we are compassionate or forgiving only some of the time, it means we are doing so at our convenience, it means we still think that there's a choice more reasonable than compassion. True compassion is not based on the cause or the action, it is simply a virtue, a response, an emotion, a feeling, we choose over any other.

I know this is not an ideal world, and in the present day and age, it almost seems that compassion or forgiveness is considered a weakness. But let's take a moment and read the following passages from the Bible. Even if you have read it numerous times before, just reread and allow it to sink in.

Pilate, wanting to release Jesus, addressed them again, but they kept shouting, "Crucify! Crucify Him!"

A third time he said to them, "Why? What has this man done wrong? I have found in Him no grounds for the death penalty. Therefore, I will have Him whipped and then release Him."

But they kept up the pressure, demanding with loud voices that He be crucified. And their voices won out. So Pilate decided to grant their demand and released the one they were asking for, who had been thrown into prison for rebellion and murder. But he handed Jesus over to their will. (Luke 23:20 – 25)

Two other criminals were also led away to be executed with Him. When as they arrived at the place called The Skull, they crucified Him there, along with the criminals, one on the right and one on the left. Then Jesus said, "Father, forgive them, because they do not know what they are doing." And they divided His clothes and cast lots.

The people stood watching, and even the leaders kept

scoffing: "He saved others; let Him save Himself if this is God's Messiah, the Chosen One!" The soldiers also mocked Him. (Luke 23:32 – 36)

"Father, forgive them, because they do not know what they are doing." This was what Jesus of Nazareth said in response to the excruciating and fatal pain he was inflicted. This was his reply to the injustice done to him. And, what happened next? "And they divided His clothes and cast lots."

Those who had mocked him, those who had put a crown of thorns on his head, those who had nailed him on the cross... Jesus forgave them. But, this was not enough, because blinded by power and greed, they threw a dice to see which solider would get what part of Christ's clothing.

There, in the same picture, you have the two extremes of our world. On the one hand is the compassion of Christ demonstrating there's no limit to how high you can rise above what you are subjected to, and on the other hand is the greed, ignorance and cruelty of the soldiers showing there's no end to how low one can stoop.

Throughout the history of our race, good people have been ridiculed and mocked, they have been jeered at, spat at, unjustly punished, beaten, even killed. Someone asked me once that what purpose did their sacrifice solve?

"Well," I said, "because Christ sacrificed his life, more than a billion people lead a life of inspiration today, even 2000 years later. Because Buddha sacrificed his kingdom, more than 500 million derive the benefit even today."

Compassion and forgiveness are simply synonyms of sacrifice. When you forgive, somewhere you sacrifice a part of your own existence, your respect, your dignity, yourself. But, by forgiving you also go beyond the shackles of ego. Besides, sacrifice is not a trade, you don't expect anything for yourself in return, it is philanthropy, it's an act of charity.

Ask me not what if the other person doesn't deserve your compassion or what if they don't acknowledge it. Because if you still have these questions, you've not let the passion of Christ sink into your heart. Allow it. Reread the passages above, do it as many times as you need or till a tear trickles down and you'll know what I mean.

A young man was mugged, beaten and left for dead on a street.

As he lay there bruised, wounded and unconscious, a man passing by, who happened to be a psychiatrist, rushed to the victim and exclaimed, "My goodness, whoever did this really needs help!"

One needs assistance and the other compassion. Either way, they both need help. In our example, if the victim is not offered help, he may die and if the culprit is not extended help, he may kill someone else. At any rate, it's a loss to our world.

The Upanishads have a term for our world — *Vashudhaiva Kutumbakam* (*Mahopanishad* VI.71-73), the whole world is one single family. It's one planet, one world, one family. Let's do our part.

Compassion does not require a reason or reward, only a desire, a discipline. Forgiveness doesn't even need discipline but only a big heart, big enough to absorb their mistakes. When your heart is as big as the ocean, their shark-like mistakes and tuna-like presence in your life will coexist without so much as causing a ripple in your mind.

# THE SEED OF DIVINITY

---

The tree laden with fruits always bends down a bit. On the path of divinity, it represents a key virtue.

---

LEGEND HAS IT THAT the king of Kazakhstan sent his royal messenger to the emperor of India, Jalal ud-din Muhammad Akbar, with three profound questions. Akbar's *nava-ratna*, or the nine jewels, were nine people of extraordinary talents. One of them was Birbal, known for his wit and wisdom. The king wanted to hear the answers in person, so, Birbal was seen off to deliver the same.

"Where does God live?" the king of Kazakhstan asked his first question.

Birbal demanded a glass of milk in response. As soon as he got it, he dipped his fingers in the glass and started rubbing them.

"Hmm…" he said shaking his head. "There's no butter in this milk."

Everyone in the court laughed out loud, and then the king said, "You have to churn milk to get cream. Further, cream must be churned to extract butter."

"Exactly, Your Excellency," Birbal said. "The butter is in the milk but we can't see it. The milk has to undergo a certain process before we can taste butter. Similarly, God lives in all living beings but an individual has to purify himself to experience the presence of God. He has to churn his consciousness and erase his ignoble thoughts, feelings and desires, to extract the divinity."

"Very well," said the king, pleased with the answer. "What does God eat?"

A hush fell over the court.

"Clearly, if God lives, then he must eat something, too," he added.

"Indeed, Your Majesty," Birbal replied instantly. "God does eat. He feasts on the false pride us humans have. Our history bears a witness to this. Eventually everyone is brought to justice in the divine court of law. Anyone who seeks God has to offer his ego."

"Beautiful!" exclaimed the king. "And, what does God do?"

"To answer this question, you'll have to come closer to me," Birbal said.

The king was taken aback at the instruction, but curious to find the answer, he stepped down from his throne and went where Birbal was standing.

"I can only answer your question by sitting on your throne," Birbal said bowing his head.

The courtiers frowned at the suggestion and nervous whispers ran through the court.

"So be it," the king said. "I must find the answer."

With utmost grace, Birbal climbed the regal staircase and

sat on the throne, a place where no one other than the king had ever seated.

Resting his hands on the two diamond-studded armrests, Birbal spoke like an emperor, "This is what God does, O king! In an instant, an ordinary mortal like me, born in a poor family, gets to be the king, where, on the other hand, you, a born king, is dethroned with least resistance."

"You've proven beyond doubt, Birbal, that the wittiest man on earth serves in Akbar's court."

The king rewarded him amply and Birbal was given a royal farewell.

By citing this story, I don't mean to say that some "person" is calling the shots up there. I leave that to your individual belief. I shared it here because the first time I'd come across this story, I absolutely enjoyed the deep philosophy and witty answers of Birbal.

I thought you might, too. Somewhere in Birbal's answers, particularly the first one, there is great truth though.

Every now and then, people ask me that how to feel God's presence in their lives. I tell them to be grateful for what all they have been blessed with, because gratitude is the quickest antidote of negativity. And when you are positive and grateful, everything in this world looks divine. But, how to experience the divinity on a more constant basis? I say practice compassion consciously. But, it's not easy, they say. Then, I suppose, the only way out is to undergo self-purification. The more you purify yourself, the greater sensitivity you develop to perceive what normally lies outside human perception.

Leading a virtuous life and a regular practice of meditation can purify anyone. Adopting virtues are even more important than meditation or any religious practice. Having said that, meditation does strengthen your mind, it makes you more mindful, so that you can stand up to your principles in the face of temptations (and there will be many). But, my focus today is not meditation. Instead, it is humility, for, humility is the seed of divinity.

Overcome with spiritual ecstasy, an archbishop approached the altar in great rush. He got down on his knees and cried, "I'm nobody, Lord! I'm nobody! Nobody!"

The bishop in attendance saw the extraordinary humility and devotional sentiment of the archbishop. Overwhelmed with love for God, he, too, ran to the altar yelling, "Lord, I'm nobody! I'm nobody, Lord!" It so happened that a janitor was mopping the floor nearby. He saw how two deeply religious people were one with God. He got goose bumps witnessing the scene. Filled with piety and a fervent spirit, he dropped his mop and dashed to the altar, proclaiming, "I'm nobody! Oh Lord, hear me, I'm nobody! Nobody!"

The archbishop took notice, turned to the bishop and said, "Look, who thinks he's nobody!"

False humility fails all spiritual tests. There's no room for exhibitionism and vanity on the divine path.

Guru Nanak differentiates most beautifully between false external humility versus true inner humility. I quote:

mithatu nīvī nānakā guṇa caṃgiāīā tatu ||

sabhu ko nivai āpa kau para kau nivai na koi ||

dhari tārājū tolīai nivai su gaurā hoi ||

aparādhī dūṇā nivai jo haṃtā miragāhi ||

sīsi nivāiai kiā thīai jā ridai kusudhe jāhi ||1||

(Sri Guru Granth Sahib, Pg 470, Salok mėhlā 1.)

Sweetness and humility, O Nanak, are the essence of virtue and goodness.

Everyone bows down to himself; no one bows down to another.

When you weigh it on the scale, the heavier side is always lower.

The sinner, like the deer hunter, bows down twice as much.

But what can be achieved by bowing the head, when the heart is impure? ||1||

As you begin to shed your ego, you become humble naturally. And humility, I may add, is the foremost prerequisite to imbibe the presence of God in your everyday life. Without humility, one can't have any more than a dry intellectual understanding or a rigid belief about God. Humility was the hallmark of the greatest saints, prophets and messiahs. Like ordinary mortals, they walked among us and quietly continued with their work.

The tree laden with fruits is always a bit bent. Not because of any burden but because it has something to offer. Humility of conduct and speech take you closer to God. The more you have to offer, the humbler you become. In the same storm where mighty winds topple giant trees, the humble blades of grass dance and sway unharmed.

# MUSINGS

# THE GREATEST SKILL

---

Your path to happiness may be influenced by various colors of life, but ultimately, it's solely carved by you.

---

DO YOU KNOW WHAT is the greatest skill to master? A skill that has no downside, the one that makes you a better person and this world a better place. Most certainly it is not the ability to accumulate a lot of knowledge or wealth. It is not about being good or great at managing relationships either. It is not the art of keeping others happy. It is not even about discovering your true nature. You may wonder what is it then.

In a certain village lived an old man who was always grumpy and cranky. No one in the community wanted to have anything to do with him because he was eternally complaining. It was said that nothing or no one could make him happy. And sadness is a like an undesirable scent, you know. Even if one person in a group puts it on, you smell it too. Rub off them and you'll reek of the same odor. The old man smelled of sadness and was as good as abandoned.

It all changed when one morning people saw him taking a stroll sporting a bright smile. This was as unusual as unexpected. He greeted others, he exchanged pleasantries and he caressed the young spikelets as he walked past the golden wheat fields. Everything about him seemed different. Some more days passed and yet his happiness didn't disappear or even diminish.

"What happened to you?" the villagers asked him one day. "We'd never seen you this happy earlier?"

"I'm eighty years old," he replied. "All my life I'd been chasing happiness. It didn't take me anywhere. I bought bigger farms, I saved more money. I tried chasing it in wealth, family, friends, power. But it always eluded me.

"One day I thought of happiness as an attractive friend. And I realized that if I had to chase in a friendship, then it wasn't worth it. I must make myself so worthy that either happiness would come after me or I would learn to live without it. I made up my mind to just enjoy whatever life brought me. The moment I decided that, happiness sneaked up on me. It's a feeling that doesn't leave me now."

We are eternally chasing happiness, like a hungry dog follows the scent of food. We think happiness is a possession and we can just own it and keep it safe. It is an erroneous view though, it's like trying to see butter in milk without churning it. This leads me to my topic today. The greatest skill, in my view, is learning to be happy on your own. If not all the time, at least majority of the time then.

You may say that being with so-and-so person makes me happy, or loving someone and being loved back makes me happy. You may even say that success makes me happy and so on. But, for how long and at whose terms? When I talk about happiness as a skill, I think more of gymnastics than soccer, for example. In the latter, you are affected by how others deal with you on the field. They may not pass you the ball or give you any opportunity to score.

When it comes to happiness, life is not a soccer field. It's a gymnastics floor and you are the gymnast. There may be a panel of judges who will be scrutinizing your moves, there may be an audience who will cheer for you, but, ultimately, your success depends on the grace and agility of your movements. It depends on how skilled you are, how well you have practiced and championed the art of gymnastics. You are solely responsible for the quality of your performance.

A popular quote paraphrased from *The Nicomachean Ethics* by Aristotle says:

Whatever we learn to do, we learn by actually doing it; men become builders, for instance, by building, and harp players by playing the instrument. In the same way, by doing just acts we become just; by doing self-controlled acts, we come to be self-controlled; and by doing brave acts, we become brave.

If there is only one skill you could master, then make it how to keep yourself happy regardless of what's going on around you. Contentment is the mother of happiness. But, if you can't feel contented for any reason, then devote yourself to a purpose or a cause that gives you a sense of fulfillment. If you don't have a purpose, then find one. It'll be worth every effort. Take my word for it. Above all, happiness is not a blessing, it is a skill. It is not something we are born with, it is something we learn.

Oscar Wilde had once said, "Some people cause happiness wherever they go; others whenever they go." Which one are you? I'm not talking about your impact on others. You may or may not be able to bring joy to them, for their happiness is more dependent on their preferences than your offerings. I'm referring to happiness in an individual context; I'm alluding to your impact on yourself. Are you happy in your own company? This is the skill of happiness.

We sit with our threads of thoughts and knit patterns of life like a knitter purls yarn. In doing so, some of us, most of us, in fact, make it too complicated. Our patterns are unnecessarily complex, and our weaving tiresome. The more we learn to appreciate the beauty in simple motifs, the easier our life becomes. Profound happiness is found in simple patterns.

What are you weaving? Pay attention, if you will.

# DEALING WITH SELF-DOUBT

A bogey or a birdie; bunker, or, an ocean
of opportunities, you won't know till you play.
What's your fear?

SELF-DOUBT—MOST HAVE IT some of the time and some have it most of the time. It is a byproduct of fear — fear of failure, of losing, of non-achievement. It is not always something you can just brush aside. Sometimes, it is borne out of a reasonable conclusion, a logical construct, a valid assessment. It may well be a state of mind acquired after cogitation. Ignoring your fear does not dispel it. False assurance does not remove the possibility of failure, and lack of success in your endeavor will lead to deeper fear and greater self-doubt. So, what causes self-doubt and what can you do about it? Keep reading. The process of winning over your fears, eliminating your self-doubt depends on the type and basis of such doubt. Without further ado, let me decipher and categorize it for you. Self-doubt can fall in one of the three non-exclusive categories:

## 1. Based on Non-Action

For example, a university student did not pay attention to his studies, he lagged behind in his coursework, and in a week from now are his exams. He is rushing to cover his syllabus but remains worried and doubtful about passing the exams. He sits down to study but can no longer concentrate or persist because he has developed this fear of failure.

Well, he has given himself every reason to develop self-doubt. In fact, it is not just that but his intelligent mind warning him. Chances are, under the ordinary circumstances, he is not going to pass his exam. He cannot regain his confidence by artificially consoling or pacifying his mind, a false assurance can only take you so far, ultimately, the reality is going to raise its head.

The best way to overcome self-doubt of this type is to sincerely work towards your goal. Observe, learn, adapt, adopt, understand, persevere, do what you have to do to stay course, to hold your fort. Actions bring results. It is action alone that will lead you to your goal, and like they say, nothing motivates like success. With practice, you attain perfection.

Practice. Persistence. Patience. If you work on these three, self-doubt will leave you forever, in the potent presence of success, it promptly loses its existence.

## 2. Based on Past Experience

A sense of self-doubt based on your past is a common scenario. Each time you fail, you register an emotion, an experience in your mind. Millions of years of evolution has transformed human mind to cling to negative emotions and fears. Some do it more than others. I do not know of anybody who never failed. Some get back to action and attain success, eliminating their fear, while many hold onto their failures limiting themselves from exploring their full potential.

Conscious mind is calculative. It is analytical. That is how humans have risen to the top of the food chain and that is the reason they have developed conscious and conditioned fears. I will elaborate on this term another day.

For example, let us say, years ago, you tried to lose weight. You were supposed to control your diet and spend four hours at the gym every week. Disregarding the discipline, you did not work as planned, you went to the gym for six days in a row one week and only once the next. The weighing scale did not budge from its original reading. You started to lose interest and began doubting if you would ever be able to lose weight. And one day, you gave up and went back to your old lifestyle, causing even more damage to your physical and mental well-being.

When you allow yourself to fail, you weaken your mind, especially if you were not honest with yourself. Fear, doubt and other negative emotions thrive inside a weak mind. If your sense of self-doubt is based on your failure in the past, all you have to do is reflect on the reasons of your failure. If you do not repeat the past actions, past results will not manifest. History can only repeat itself if you start living a historical present.

Albert Einstein once said: "Insanity is to keep doing the same thing, expecting different results."

## 3. Based on Innate Fear

Self-doubt based on fear is more common when one wants to tread the unknown waters; some even have the ripe opportunity, but they are either settled in their comfort zone or too afraid to try anything new. The latter is my present focus.

Ability to take risks varies in each individual. If you have been contemplating on embarking on a new venture, trying something different, but self-doubt and fear of failure keeps holding you back, you can only address them by contemplation and coming up with a strategy. If you are keen on learning how to swim, eventually, you have to jump in the water. There comes a time when you have to let go off the floaters and swim on your own.

The best way to overcome fear-based self-doubt is to write down your answers to the following questions:

a.  Why do I want change?

b.  Am I ready to embrace change?

c.  What is the worst that can happen?

d.  Do I feel competent enough to handle the worst?

Reflect on your answers, prioritize and act accordingly.

When you experience self-doubt, get to its root to remove it. Do not just ignore it, especially if it persists. It could just be your fear or it may well be your intuitive faculty guiding you. You will only know the truth upon self-reflection. And I reiterate, the most potent question you can ask yourself to overcome self-doubt is: what is the worst that can happen?

Take it easy. Do not spend your time brooding over your past, over-anticipating your future or making elaborate plans devoid of action. It is a precious life, do something priceless with it.

# THE ONLY THING YOU NEED TO KNOW

---

Conduct yourself in a manner that befits you — at all times, under all circumstances, with everyone.

---

PERHAPS, WHAT I'VE SHARED in here is the only thing you ever need to know. Yeah, I know it's a tall claim, but hopefully, by the time you get to the end of this chapter, you'll have a new perspective. Many readers who read my memoir ask me that how come I was (or am) not angry with my guru. They question why did I go through what I did at his place. I will give you my answer in one simple sentence: I don't see how having grudges against anyone or holding anger regarding anything does any good to anybody. I stayed at his place out of choice, maybe even a naive one, yet it was a conscious choice. And I must take complete responsibility for my own choices.

Because, ultimately, we are responsible for our conduct. When you drop the veil of ego, of I-ness, there's no distinction. The same Divine dwells in all. Each one of us is an identical entity in the infinite creation, like drops in the ocean.

Before I spell out the most important thing you ever need to know in my view, here's a short poem called *The Paradoxical Commandments* by American writer Kent M Keith, which is sometimes attributed to Mother Teresa, for this was hung on a wall in a children's home where she served for the most part of her life.

The version I share below is slightly modified from the original one and is more commonly referred to as *The Final Analysis*.

People are often unreasonable, illogical, and self-centered,
Forgive them anyway.
If you are kind, people may accuse you of selfish, ulterior motives,
Be kind anyway.
If you are successful, you will win some false friends and some true friends,
Succeed anyway.
If you are honest and frank, people may cheat you,
Be honest and frank anyway.
What you spend years building, someone could destroy overnight,
Build anyway.
If you find serenity and happiness, they may be jealous,
Be happy anyway.
The good you do today, people will often forget tomorrow,
Do good anyway.
Give the world your best anyway.
You see, in the final analysis, it is not between you and them,
It is between you and God.
It was never between you and them anyway.

We are often dealing with conflicting situations in life. Every now and then we have to make choices, choices that affect our present and shape our future. No doubt, actions and choices of our parents, family members and others around us have an impact on our lives, too. The truth, however, remains that our life is mostly the outcome of *our* thoughts and actions and not others'. And, choices are not always black-or-white; the path is not always clear.

The question is how should we behave when we are being wronged or mistreated? Should we not give it back to the other person when we know for sure that they are being unreasonable? Or should we follow M K Gandhi's turn-the-other-cheek formula?

Here's my view. We suffer when we hold other people responsible for our choices. We suffer when we think the world owes us something. For most things we want in life, from wealth and status to love and respect, we have to earn it. No one owes us anything. Yes, yes, I know, you may say: but what if I have done a lot for someone, shouldn't they have any duty of care towards me? Maybe. The fact is, they are responsible for their actions and you for yours. We can't say that we mistreated them because they did the same to us.

There was a man once who took out a Rs. 5,000 loan. Out of this sum, he lent Rs. 4,000 to a friend who needed it urgently. The remaining Rs. 1,000 he used for his personal stuff. A month later, the bank manager asked for a repayment.

"Is it okay if I just pay an installment on Rs. 1,000 and not on the whole amount because I only used Rs. 1,000?" he asked the manager. "My friend borrowed the rest."

The manager was not pleased. "Look, I gave the loan to you and I'm not responsible for what you did with it. I need the repayment on the full sum," he said.

Similarly, in the final analysis, nature will say, "I gave you the body and mind and what you did with it was your responsibility." At that moment, you can't say, "I wronged because I was wronged." For, it'll say, "What they did is their business, I'll talk to them separately. I'm only concerned with your account." Figuratively speaking, of course. We can't take other people's wrongdoing as any justification for our own misconduct. Each one of us is accountable for the transactions in our karmic account.

Finally, let me tell you the only thing you ever need to know. Here: in any situation, you should behave in a manner that befits you. You follow this principle and you'll know right from wrong; you'll know what choice to make. When they elicit anger, hate or other negative emotions in you, at that time, ask yourself a simple question: if I could make a completely independent choice, unaffected by the conduct and actions of the other person, how would I behave? Almost always, you will find that you *can* behave in your way; you don't have to carry yourself any differently. The pure ones, the noble ones, don't cast stones irrespective of the actions of the other person. Besides, violent thoughts, words and actions only grow and never diminish when returned with violence. Violence is not Swami's way.

Conduct yourself in a manner that befits you. At all times, under all circumstances, with everyone. Now, go ahead and reflect on what kind of behavior suits someone of your stature. Done? Live it.

This is the only thing you ever need to know. The only mantra. Rest is commentary.

# THE PATH TO SUCCESS

---

How long will it take to get there is not always
dependent on the speed alone.

---

I ONCE READ SOMEWHERE: nothing motivates like success. It
is often the desire to succeed, to derive joy from attainment
of a goal and the benefits from such achievement that drive
individuals to persist and persevere, to toil and tolerate. As
a race, we are designed to feel motivated by thinking about
the end result.

You tell someone they are hired for a job, paying them one
hundred grand a year, and they immediately start visualizing
saving or spending that money; they start planning, they start
imagining themselves in the office, speaking to co-workers
and the rest of it. It is natural. Steadily, these thoughts become
part of one's expectations. If what they thought varies greatly
from what they actually get, they are disappointed. They set a
goal for themselves, the next target and they give themselves
a time frame. So far so good.

Whenever embarking on a new venture though, the primary
difference between success and failure is the motivation to

persist. A winner chooses to carry on. When people quiz me about meditation, changing their habits, about self-realization and so forth, the one common question I get is: how long will it take? Let me share a little story with you.

An elderly monk was en route to an ancient temple in the mountains. Traveling on foot, he had been on this pilgrimage for nearly two months now. In the spirit of a monk, he carried with him no possessions except his alms-bowl and a set of robes. He would simply stop whenever he felt like resting and beg for food whenever he was hungry.

One step at a time, he traveled over two thousand kilometers. Finally, the tall mountain with a temple like a crown on its head was visible from a distance. A feeling of relief, a surge of joy, a sense of accomplishment rose up his spine.

A further few steps and he saw an old woman working in the fields. He stopped and asked, "How long will it take me to reach the temple at the top of the mountain?"

The old woman turned around to face him, gave him an indifferent stare, shrugged and went back to her work. The monk thought it was highly unusual because he knew most villagers to be friendly and warm-hearted. *Perhaps the woman did not hear me*, he thought. Pointing in the direction of the temple, he repeated, "How long will it take me to reach that shrine?"

The woman gave the same reaction again. But this time, she softly growled, too. The monk asked his question one more time only to get the same response. He concluded that the old woman was deaf. A little disappointed, he resumed walking towards the mountain.

"It'll take you eight hours," a voice yelled from behind. It was the old woman.

Intrigued, the monk walked back to her and said, "I don't get it. I asked you three times and you did not answer me. Now that I was on my way, you called me from behind to tell me the distance."

"I'm not telling you the distance, Master. I'm simply telling you how long it will take *you*," she spoke, "when you asked me earlier you were standing still. How could have I answered your question without knowing how fast you walk! As for the distance, from here it's a trek of twenty miles."

There you are! There is no absolute answer to how long it will take you. It depends on multiple factors and your pace is only one of them. More often than not, it is just about staying the course. We all know the hare and the tortoise classic.

There are essentially four elements that lead to success. They are:

1. **Knowledge:** Are you well-equipped? Mentally and skill-wise? If not, what do you need to do to acquire it?

2. **Approach:** Do you have the right mindset and approach? Are you positive, optimistic, ready, flexible?

3. **Resources:** Do you have the right tools, resources, or are you trying to drill a hole in the wall with a spoon?

4. **Efforts:** Are you putting your best foot forward no matter what?

However, there is a fifth element. You can call it grace, fate, luck, destiny or anything else you wish. This one manifests when you do not waver from your path. It may appear like a coincidence, a stint of luck or serendipity, but the truth is, with the four elements above, you create that perfect moment of realization, of attainment.

Steady and small steps turn into giant strides and leaps ultimately. Tiny drops of water, one after the other, create a waterfall. Buddha did not gain enlightenment just because he sat under the Bodhi tree; he slogged for years before the arrival of that perfect moment; all that learning and struggle culminated to manifest the moment of revelation, of epiphany, before prince Gautama became Buddha.

Go on! Give it your best shot. You should be able to look in the mirror and say, "I gave it my best shot and I tried everything I possibly could." When you can say that to yourself honestly, you can have your wildest dreams come true — from material success to divine realization.

# FREEDOM

The sky remains independent of the colors and clouds in it. It returns to its natural state — blue. So can you.

WHERE DO YOU GO when you want answers? Answers to such questions as what is right or wrong, how am I looking, how am I performing, what is good or bad, or even, what is moral and what is immoral, am I on the right track, will God hate me if I do this or that. What if you could source answers from within? Must someone else validate our opinions? It is normal to feel comforted with external affirmations. We feel reassured when others confirm our own beliefs. But it need not be this way. If you want, and if you are willing to work towards it, you can transcend others' opinions and affirmations. And what does working towards it entail, you may ask. There are two things that will lead you to that exalted state, first, self-contemplation, and second, inner strength.

## Self-Contemplation

Self-contemplation is the art of understanding yourself better, it is knowing why and how you do whatever you do. We all have motivations behind our actions. Most of the time, our motivations live in our subconscious. Self-contemplation helps you bring them to the forefront. In the words of Ralph Ellison:

> *All my life I had been looking for something, and everywhere I turned someone tried to tell me what it was. I accepted their answers too, though they were often in contradiction and even self-contradictory. I was naive. I was looking for myself and asking everyone except myself questions which I, and only I, could answer. It took me a long time and much painful boomeranging of my expectations to achieve a realization everyone else appears to have been born with: that I am nobody but myself.*

Who can know you better than you? You alone know your innermost thoughts, actions and intentions. The more you understand yourself, the closer you get to your primordial source of strength and divinity. No doubt it requires a certain degree of inner strength and that leads to the second attribute. Read on.

## Inner Strength

The sole purpose of my writings is to help you understand yourself better, transform yourself, to be yourself. It is all about you that I am concerned with. What do you need to do in order to build that impeccable and undying inner strength? I could write pages and pages on it, hundreds of verses I could quote from various religious texts. Instead, I am choosing to share with you a poem by the famous British writer and poet, Rudyard Kipling. The poem is aptly titled *If*.

If you can keep your head when all about you
Are losing theirs and blaming it on you;
If you can trust yourself when all men doubt you,
But make allowance for their doubting too:
If you can wait and not be tired by waiting,
Or, being lied about, don't deal in lies,
Or being hated don't give way to hating,
And yet don't look too good, nor talk too wise;

If you can dream — and not make dreams your master;
If you can think — and not make thoughts your aim,
If you can meet with Triumph and Disaster
And treat those two impostors just the same:.
If you can bear to hear the truth you've spoken
Twisted by knaves to make a trap for fools,
Or watch the things you gave your life to, broken,
And stoop and build'em up with worn-out tools;

If you can make one heap of all your winnings
And risk it on one turn of pitch-and-toss,
And lose, and start again at your beginnings,
And never breathe a word about your loss:
If you can force your heart and nerve and sinew
To serve your turn long after they are gone,
And so hold on when there is nothing in you
Except the Will which says to them: "Hold on!"

If you can talk with crowds and keep your virtue,
Or walk with Kings — nor lose the common touch,
If neither foes nor loving friends can hurt you,
If all men count with you, but none too much:

If you can fill the unforgiving minute
With sixty seconds' worth of distance run,
Yours is the Earth and everything that's in it,
And — which is more — you'll be a Man, my son!

Living a mindful life, whenever you are gripped by anger, paranoia, insecurity, at that moment, if you can remind yourself of the promises you made to yourself, if you can focus on the code of conduct you have set for yourself, you are well on your way to be a superman (or superwoman) of your inner world. Without having to do hours and hours of meditation, without the support of some grand theory, without subjugation to any religious authority, you would gain exceptional freedom of thought. You will become independent. Independent of others' opinions, affirmations, treatment and conduct.

Independent — it means you are only *Dependent* on what is *In* you. That is freedom.

# WHY DO PEOPLE LAUGH?

Mary had a little lamb. What? She gave birth to a lamb? Everyone was expecting a human baby!

LAUGHTER IS ONE OF the most fundamental human expressions and a sense of humor is nothing short of divinity. Ever wonder why do we laugh? The roots of laughter go deeper than you might think. One's laughter can reveal much about the person, culture, race or group. There are those who can laugh at others, at situations, at themselves. My focus today is on why people laugh at a joke.

Our race has evolved, grown and adjusted based on the principle of consistency. For thousands of years, our ancestors lived in the caves. They did not change, they did not need to or so they felt. Every time someone caused a disruption with an invention or a discovery, we made another step towards something new, another step away from the norm. Change is rarely welcomed upon its introduction. People feel intimidated with change; they are threatened with the fear of unknown.

Laughing at a joke is no different. A joke begins with a normal scenario, the type you are comfortable with, the one you find consistent with your belief system. And suddenly, a conflicting situation is presented to you, it is unexpected, unprecedented — there is a change. A certain level of tension builds up, it defies your logic. Subconsciously, you know there is no threat. So, your mind releases the tension with peals of laughter. The patterns in your brain get rearranged causing laughter without tickling, so to speak.

For example, consider the following:

"Mary had a little lamb..."

She found it a bit too spicy.

When you tell this joke to children, they laugh much more. Why? They are quick to release tension arising from a conflicting viewpoint, a sudden surprise. An adult on the other hand might have been introduced to more conflicting situations during the course of his own life. He can live with the unfamiliar ending of Mary actually eating her lamb; he couldn't be bothered; it does not create a tension in his head, he's been through much more. It does not tickle his funny bone as much as it does a child's.

You do not laugh upon a release of tension if you perceive a threat though. Imagine, someone appears in front of you suddenly, pulls out a gun from his pocket and shoots in your direction. You are convinced you are shot. You promptly frisk your body to look for wounds and blood, but there is nothing, not even a mark. Further imagine, he is playing a prank. You are unlikely to laugh at this one immediately. Because, you experienced a certain threat. The conflict between life and death was not just an intellectual proposition, it felt real. The tension was a little too much for you. Upon realizing you are safe, you are more likely to sigh than break into a giggle. However, fast forward to a few weeks or months, you may look back at the whole incident and find yourself laughing. Why? Because the underlying threat has disappeared.

Is life not all about conflicting and contrasting situations? Not all situations need to be taken seriously; you can laugh many of them out. How to rise above that threat? Examine it. If you can analyze it, you can take the right action, you can then focus on the right thought and the threat dispels automatically thereafter. Fear is always out of anticipation. There is no fear in the present moment; it is in the anticipation of what may happen in the next or subsequent moments.

The more your mind can handle conflict, the less you laugh at ordinary jokes. The greater the number of your experiences in life, the fewer the jokes that can make you laugh. Through your struggles, your experiences and evolved intellect, life teaches you to accept situations that defy logic, that are highly contrasting, inherently conflicting. You can easily know a great deal about a person from a. the way they laugh, b. the type of jokes they laugh at, and c. at what and who all they laugh at.

Children or childlike people can laugh at simple gestures; they can giggle at jokes with no meaning. Similarly, if you become childlike, living in the world becomes a whole lot easier, it gets more interesting. How to be childlike, you ask? Practice compassion and gratitude. It's also okay to cry and complain like them sometimes. *Sometimes.*

In a village lived an old man, wise and content. Amidst a group of people, he cracked a funny joke. Everyone laughed. After a silence of a few minutes, he told the same joke again. Fewer laughed this time. He let another few minutes pass and cracked but the same joke again. No one laughed. Most thought the old man had gone cuckoo.

"You can't laugh at the same joke more than a couple of times," he said, "yet you keep crying over the same problems all your life."

What if you actually realized that conflicting situations in life are there to make you laugh? What if this whole world, this universe is simply a prank, a play, a joke? Either way, laughing it out is better than brooding over it. It is more enjoyable that way. It is a choice. Yours for the taking.

"Forgive, O Lord, my little jokes on Thee and I'll forgive Thy great big one on me." ~Robert Frost

Laughter means you are comfortable. Go on! Make someone laugh today, it will give you joy.

# The Source of Your Wisdom

---

Rocks of opinions sit there gathering moss of
emotions and distorting your view of reality.
They hinder your growth.

---

I REMEMBER READING THIS real life story by writer Pablo Valle
once. He was in Japan conducting English classes. Winter
was fast approaching and as it happens during the change
of seasons, many people were contracting cold and flu. On a
cold morning, a Japanese student walked into his class with
her mouth covered. She was wearing a surgical mask. Pablo
thought, *Wow, people would go to extremes not to get sick in this
country*. An hour later, during a short break, he approached
her.

"Why the mask?" he scoffed. "Are you so afraid of catching
cold?"

"Not quite," she said. "In Japan, you use it when you are
under the weather and you don't want other people to get sick.
It is the polite thing to do."

Pablo was as embarrassed as stunned and called it a
lesson he would never forget. The truth is, like Pablo, we are

constantly forming our opinions about other traditions and people based on a set of assumptions that are rarely correct, based on a view, which is often biased. What is the basis of our knowledge, after all? We are so conditioned and sometimes so [over] confident about what we think we know that we categorize and label other people without even realizing it. In simple words, our premature conclusions often lack reason and substance.

Personally, I like to classify stereotypes into positive and negative. They both are equally damaging though, because when we form an opinion not based on facts but on a fixed set of ideas we have in our head, our own behavior undergoes a dramatic shift.

For example, late into the evening, you spot a few black youth with a loudly playing boombox in a park and you immediately worry for your own safety. They could be MBA students from Harvard or even undercover police officers, but a stereotypical mind loses its sense of judgment and understanding. It jumps to conclusion far too quickly.

Once we form a view about someone based on our assumptions, our own thought patterns shift almost immediately. We judge people based on how they look, talk, act, walk, etc. We are eternally categorizing them based on their race, religion, color, and so on. And, even though you may not be aware, these stereotypes — positive or negative — weaken your own sense of self-worth and self-esteem. How, you may wonder. Keep reading.

Positive stereotypes instill a sense of fear and submission in you. For instance, when we meet someone with authority, wealth or status, we quickly conclude that this person must command our respect; that, somehow this person is better than I am and therefore, I must exercise submission. Or, we may assign a negative stereotype leading to fear, jealousy, hatred or envy. For example, we may think that the rich person must be bad, or the powerful politician must be a liar, or the man in robes must be a fanatic and so on.

Either way, stereotypes don't let you explore life. They greatly limit you and your potential. Our conventional ideas about others severely restrict our freedom to better enjoy and understand our own world. They give us a distorted view of truth. Look at the history of our race — the only people who changed the world were the ones who challenged the conventions. A Martin Luther King, a Mother Teresa, a Gandhi, an Einstein, a Darwin, was born because somewhere they didn't just subscribe to the stereotypes, but instead, listened to their inner voice.

Not all Hindus are tolerant, nor all Muslims rigid; not all Catholics are staunch, nor all Jews orthodox. Not all rich are snobs, nor all poor kind; not all politicians are liars, nor all lawyers dishonest. Unless you get to spend time with someone, or have the opportunity to observe them closely, any opinion you form about them is likely to be based on an assumption or some preconceived notion, and not the actual reality. If you really think about it, no one gains anything by forming a negative stereotype. It only breeds hatred and anger.

An English passenger was traveling in the London Underground when a man of Arabic appearance got off the train, leaving a bag behind. Suspecting something fishy, the Englishman grabbed the bag and chased the owner. Soon, catching up with him, he nervously thrust the bag in the owner's hands.

The man thanked him profusely and reached into his bag, which appeared to contain bundles of banknotes. He offered him a reward, which the polite English refused.

The Arab looked around furtively and then murmured, "While I can't repay your kindness, sir, I will give you a word of advice. Stay away from The American Diner on Coventry Street."

Terrified, the English whispered, "Is there going to be an attack?"

"No," he whispered back. "The food is shit and the desserts are horrible."

Next time, you judge someone based on their appearance, attire, race or any other external factor, just pause for a moment. Trust me, it'll be worth it. Just get to know them personally before you think you know them already. And this is what a stereotype is in a nutshell: thinking that you know them without knowing them at all. Remind yourself to not box people based on what you think you know about them. I'm not saying you don't have the right to an opinion. You do. But, form it based on your own experience, based on first-hand information, and not on a bunch of preconceived notions.

This will help you keep your head empty, your heart light and your mind free. A smile will emerge naturally on your face. Besides, when you know other people for real, you'll realize how little you really knew them.

When you open up to someone without being judgmental, you will get to see and appreciate the world from their eyes, too. You will have helped in making our planet a better place. Being non-judgmental is also a form of compassion. And compassion melts negativity. Yes, compassion has the power to melt everything. It dissolves, it absorbs. Practice compassion to know what I mean.

# You Are Not Weak

---

Even the hard coconut can break in one blow. It doesn't mean it's weak. It's vulnerable.

---

SHOULD YOU BE STRONG all the time? Is it possible?

Be Strong — it's an expression we all have heard countless times. Since childhood. As a child when you fall down and people don't want to see you cry, they tell you to be strong. As an adult, anything untoward happens and they don't want you to cry, they tell you to be strong. A caring person will understand your plight and induce strength in you with their empathy. A weak person will convince you that you are being a coward by not being strong. A weak person cannot have empathy; the weak one wants you to ignore your challenges, they want you to hide your fears and concerns. Why? Because somewhere, they are scared themselves, they are afraid that seeing you like that may make them weaker, it may expose their own emotional mess.

While I don't deny that a certain degree of strength is needed to survive the blows life can deliver sometimes, at the same time I believe strength does not come from hiding who we are and what we are feeling. That will only be an illusion of strength. Real strength comes from being honest to yourself, it comes from acceptance and understanding.

Let me share with you a real-life story out of American scholar and author Brené Brown's *I Thought It Was Just Me*:

The author's mother's only sibling was killed in a violent shooting. Her grandmother couldn't endure the death of her son. Quoting verbatim:

> "Having been an alcoholic most of her life, my grandmother didn't have the emotional resources she needed to survive a traumatic loss like this. For weeks she roamed her neighborhood, randomly asking the same people over and over if they had heard about his death.
>
> One day, right after my uncle's memorial service, my mom totally broke down. I had seen her cry once or twice, but I certainly had never seen her cry uncontrollably. My sisters and I were afraid and crying mostly because we were so scared to see her like that. I finally told her that we didn't know what to do because we had never seen her 'so weak.' She looked at us and said, in a loving yet forceful voice, 'I'm not weak. I'm stronger than you can imagine. I'm just very vulnerable right now. If I were weak, I'd be dead.' "

Next time anyone tells you to be strong or when they say you are weak or if you feel within you are weak, recall the story above. If you are hurt, when you're injured, there's going to be a wound. You have to take care of the abrasion if you want it to heal quicker. When the wound is fresh, it's susceptible to infection and deterioration. This is vulnerability. It is a phase, a temporary state. When you experience trauma, you experience a sort of helplessness, you are not your normal self during this period, you are vulnerable. It does not mean you are a weak individual. It simply means you are recovering, it means you are human, it means you are normal.

Weakness is when you believe you are what others say about you, when you go on a pity party, when you downgrade yourself, when you start to believe you are unworthy because you are not fulfilling someone's criteria. Just because there's a misfit, it doesn't mean you are unworthy. Just because you want the other person and they don't want you as much, it doesn't mean you have to change yourself so they may want you, it doesn't mean you don't deserve them. It simply means the fit is not right there. A shoe of size seven is not unworthy of a foot of size six, it's just unfit.

Unfit does not equal unworthiness just like vulnerable is not weak. Never let anyone tag your worth.

I'm not saying we should not work on self-improvement, I'm not recommending we should ignore our shortcomings and limitations, I'm simply suggesting that you don't need to weigh yourself on someone else's rigged scale. If you believe you ought to work on an aspect of you, go ahead, but only if you truly want it. Life is not a battle, you are not in a boxing ring that you have to keep fighting and show your strength till one of the opponent's knocked out or the time runs out. Sometimes, most of the times in fact, it's perfectly fine to take a back step, to cry, to be yourself, to express yourself.

To show your emotions does not make you weak. On the contrary, it shows you are genuine. Just because a part of your life is broken doesn't mean you are weak or unworthy, it doesn't necessarily mean you are at fault. It could just be one of those times when you went out without an umbrella on a clear day but it rained cats and dogs.

If there's one gift you can give to yourself, if there's one resolution you can make to transform yourself, it could be: never let anyone ever tell you what your worth is; never let them dictate how you see yourself. Next time someone neglects your feelings and tells you to be strong instead, please know that that person is not the right one to share your feelings with. You'll be better off speaking to a mirror. Or maybe you'll get more out of it if you just call the customer care at your telephone company and insist they hear you out for the next few minutes. You've been a loyal customer for years, and the least they can do is listen to your grievance for five minutes. Alright, I'm only joking.

# THE CRACKED POT

---

Our weakness becomes our strength when we are
honest with ourselves.

---

SOMEONE WROTE TO ME asking if self-improvement is an endless
pursuit. He wrote, "Are we to keep trying forever?" He was
alluding to the fact that if we keep working on ourselves,
forever finding faults in us, when will we actually enjoy life? Is
life meant to be a drag? Are we supposed to keep seeking room
for improvement? To think about it, it is a beautiful question.

Personally, I don't believe that you need to fit into someone
else's frame of perfection. Besides, aiming for perfection is
often a matter of personal choice, an individual preference.
Perfection is subjective. What is perfect to you may not be
even half-decent for the other person. The goal is not to fulfill
the world's criteria of excellence, but to fill your own life
with grace, bliss and compassion. They are the ingredients of
a virtuous life, as perfect as it can get.

Long, long ago, there was a poor but noble man. There was
no source of water nearby his home. So, every day, he would
go down to the river carrying a stick on his shoulders with

two large pots hanging from each side of it. These pots were made from metal, and one of them was so worn it developed a crack, almost a hole, three years ago. As a result, it looked more like a percolator— drop by drop it leaked constantly. The other vessel was in perfect shape though. Each day, the man would fill both the pots to the brim, and every time the cracked pot would only be half full by the time he reached home. Once home, he would promptly transfer the water to an earthen pot.

The cracked pot felt guilty. It wanted to serve its master but was helpless as there was no way for it to fill the crack, to plug the hole. The perfect pot looked down on the cracked pot for it was aware of its own superiority. There were times when the cracked pot felt jealous of the perfect pot, but mostly it felt helpless and depressed. No matter how hard it tried, it only ever reached home half empty.

One day, when the master was by the river, the cracked pot said, "I'm a pathetic pot. I'm so sorry for I'm unable to do my job. You fill me up every day and carry home so much weight, but I never get there full like the other pot. Please forgive me, I'm so ashamed of myself. You deserve a better pot, a perfect one and not a cracked pot like me. Please sell me to the smith. Let him end my miserable and useless life. You'll get relief, too."

"Useless?" the man spoke compassionately, "I wish you knew how proud I am of you. Who doesn't have flaws? I do, too. If I could afford, I would have had you repaired long time ago, so you wouldn't feel like this today. But, then again, in our flaws lies our divinity. A sense of flawlessness is no more than a viewpoint, often an arrogant one, in fact. Have you any idea how much you've helped in beautifying this place?"

"Me? Help?" the cracked pot exclaimed, "Beautifying?"

"Yes! I would like you to observe your side of the track when we go home today."

The man began walking home and the cracked pot realized that on one side of the path, specifically on the side it was on, there were flowers, beautiful flowers, all the way. Butterflies were hovering above them, bees were buzzing on some; there was fragrance in the air.

"A while ago, I planted a new variety of flower seeds. I figured the water dripping from you could easily provide nourishment to the seeds. And now look! Not only do we have beautiful flowers but the bees have carried the pollen far and wide, and we have more and more of these flowers blooming everywhere. These ones attract bees like anything and there are more natural beehives in the village now than ever before. If not for your so-called flaw, it would not have been possible to have this beauty, fragrance and utility that we have today."

Hope you like the story as much as I did when I first came across it. The seeds of perfection are already sown in our flaws. Rather than aiming to be somebody else, instead of aspiring to be some perfect pot, it is far more important to put both our strengths and limitations to use. If you are honest about your cracks and are willing to see how they may add meaning to your own life, a whole new world of possibilities will open up.

There is nothing called absolute weakness or strength, they switch roles based on the context and need. A sturdy stick may be good as a walking support, but you need a supple one to make a bow. What is strength from one perspective is weakness from another. No matter how cracked you are, you still have a role to play.

# SPIRITUALITY

# A Story of Faith

---

Some part of our life will inevitably go in peeling
the coconut before we can enjoy the sweet water
and tender flesh inside.

---

THIS IS ONE OF my favorite stories from the great epic
*Mahabharata*. A story of faith and surrender, of destiny and
divinity. This incident happened when legions of troops from
all over the country were being mobilized to fight one of the
bloodiest battles in the history of India. The great war between
the Kauravas and the Pandavas that lasted eighteen days.

The battlefield of Kurukshetra was being prepared to
facilitate the movement of mammoth armies with large
cavalries. Areas were marked out for rival camps. Huge
bundles of wood were organized to cook food for a sea of
armies. They used elephants to uproot trees and clear the
ground. On one such tree lived a sparrow, a mother of four
young ones. As the tree was being knocked down, her nest
landed on the ground along with her offspring — too young
to fly — miraculously unharmed.

The vulnerable and frightened sparrow looked around for

help. Just then she saw Krishna scanning the field with Arjuna. They were there to physically examine the battleground and devise a winning military strategy before the onset of the war. She flapped her tiny wings with all her might to reach Krishna's chariot.

"Please save my children, O Krishna," the sparrow pleaded. "They will be crushed tomorrow when this battle starts."

"I hear you," said He, the omniscient one, "but, I can't interfere with the laws of nature."

"All I know is that you are my savior, O Lord. I rest my children's fate in your hands. You can kill them or you can save them, it's up to you now."

"The wheel of Time moves indiscriminately," Krishna spoke like an ordinary man implying that there wasn't anything he could do about it.

"I don't know any philosophy," the sparrow said with faith and reverence. "You *are* the wheel of Time. That's all I know. I surrender to thee."

"Stock food for three weeks in your nest then."

Unaware of the on-going conversation, Arjuna was trying to shoo away the sparrow when Krishna smiled at the bird. She fluttered her wings a few times in obeisance and flew back to her nest.

Two days later, just before the boom of the conchs announced the commencement of the battle, Krishna asked Arjuna for his bow and an arrow. Arjuna was startled because Krishna had vowed to not lift any weapon in the war. Besides, Arjuna believed that he was the best archer out there.

"Order me, Lord," he said with conviction, "nothing is impenetrable for my arrows."

Quietly taking the bow from Arjuna, Krishna took aim at an elephant. But, instead of bringing the animal down, the arrow hit the bell around its neck and sparks flew.

Arjuna couldn't contain his chuckle seeing that Krishna missed an easy mark.

"Should I?" he offered.

Again ignoring his reaction, Krishna gave him back the bow and said that no further action was necessary.

"But, why did you shoot at the elephant, Keshav?" Arjuna asked.

"Because this was the elephant that had knocked down the tree sheltering that sparrow's nest."

"Which sparrow?" Arjuna exclaimed. "Plus, the elephant is unhurt and alive. Only the bell is gone!"

Dismissing Arjuna's questions, Krishna instructed him to blow his conch.

The war began and numerous lives were lost over the next eighteen days. The Pandavas won in the end. Once again, Krishna took Arjuna with him to navigate through the ruddy field. Many corpses still lay there awaiting their funeral. The battleground was littered with severed limbs and heads, lifeless steeds and elephants.

Krishna stopped at a certain spot and looked down thoughtfully at an elephant-bell.

"Arjuna," he said, "will you lift this bell for me and put it aside?"

The instruction, though simple, made little sense to Arjuna. After all, in the vast field where plenty of other things needed clearing, why would Krishna ask him to move an insignificant piece of metal out of the way? He looked at him questioningly.

"Yes, this bell," Krishna reiterated. "It's the same bell that had come off the elephant's neck I had shot at."

Arjuna bent down to move the heavy bell without another question. As soon as he lifted it though, his world changed forever.

One, two, three, four and five. Four young birds flew out one after another followed by a sparrow. The mother bird swirled in circles around Krishna, circumambulating him in great joy. The one bell Krishna had cleaved eighteen days ago had protected the entire family.

"Forgive me, O Krishna," said Arjuna. "Seeing you in human body and behaving like ordinary mortals, I had forgotten who you really are."

I've always held that faith doesn't mean life will go according to you. Instead, it means that you learn to get along with life. You recognize that life must run its own course.

That your individual life is a tiny, albeit an integral part of a grand play of nature. An immensely grand play, actually.

Krishna had left the sparrow in the battlefield for it was destined to be there. The bird might have wished to be somewhere safer with her children. She could have argued with Krishna to take her family with him. She could have begged that they give her three weeks of food. But she didn't do any of those. She simply followed the instruction and left it in the hands of the one she believed in. She didn't forego the effort expected from her.

Many people see faith or surrender as a way to have their dreams come true. They believe that if they pray to some god, their wishes will be granted. This is not how nature operates. It can't afford to, for we often wish for the wrong things. We desire certain outcomes without realizing or understanding the cost of those desires. We forget that our choices are intricately linked to our fate, they shape our destiny. In wanting the "good" stuff alone, we only see what we want to see.

Rather than aiming to be the person who will keep his partner happy, we wish for a person who will keep *us* happy, for example. And as we change, things that made us happy earlier no longer appeal to us. We then wish for another person, a better partner or something on those lines. Rather than being content with what we have, we crave for more things. To acquire more things, we work harder, often at the cost of our health and relationships. The quality of living may go up but the quality of life will be compromised and then we wonder about why more things are not making us happy.

Yes, you can grow a seedless melon but not a skinless one. Nature puts a protective covering on everything. Removing that layer can be sometimes tedious or messy, but without it, the fruit will perish before it even ripens. Some part of our life will inevitably go in peeling the coconut before we can enjoy the sweet water and tender meat inside.

Faith is not a tug-of-war between your desires and His grace (both of which are endless), hoping that one day you'll lure God into playing unfair. On the contrary, faith is letting go. It is raising your hands in surrender without giving up on your action. Faith is knowing that not every day out there will be sunny. And that's okay. It is realizing that dawn *will* follow dusk. Faith is the awareness that a cloudy sky doesn't mean that the sun has set.

To work on everything that you can and to let go off everything beyond your control is faith in a nutshell. Such faith, made up of action and surrender, is the most potent antidote to all fears.

As the French scientist Blaise Pascal said most beautifully, "The heart has its reasons which reason knows nothing of... We know the truth not only by the reason, but by the heart."

Faith is heart's wisdom. It's what your mind can't grasp but your heart knows. Give it a place in your life and you'll fly with a thousand wings. Higher and swifter. Across the seas, beyond the skies.

# THE GURU

---

Just like the full moon that softly dispels the darkness,
a genuine master lights up your soul.

---

WHEN WE MAKE SOMEONE happy, the same part in our brain is activated as it does when we do something for our own happiness. This is not philosophy but neuroscience. I'm not surprised though; the joy of giving far exceeds any other I've ever known. Charity begins at home, they say. A happy environment at home is comparable to heaven on earth. In my occupation, I get to meet many people from all walks of life.

Do you know the difference between the light of the sun versus the moon's? The sun's presence annihilates any darkness whereas the moon dissipates the darkness without eliminating it completely. The moon is soothing while the sun seething. Like the moon, a guru allows you to exist the way you are, accepting you the way you are, ever exuding the gentle rays, the full light of love, care, wisdom and guidance.

The guru-disciple relationship is like no other, for it's free of the usual give-and-take exchanges. It's one of the most intimate and purest relationships because there are no secrets between the two and there's no hidden agenda. It's a bond, a covenant, capable of rapid, profound, and irreversible transformation.

In the present day and age though, while the sanctity of this relationship is as intact as it ever was, there is no dearth of examples where both the guru and the disciple abuse each other's trust and sentiments. In my vocation, I regularly meet seekers who have been prey to fake gurus. There are also fake disciples though — these get initiated but never really follow the teachings in its entirety.

That said, there are many who do follow ardently and practice sincerely yet their doubts and negative tendencies remain with them. They don't experience any transformation. Why? What are they doing wrong? When a seeker is sincere, when they follow their guru's instructions to the T but still fail to walk the spiritual path, the fault is often not with the seeker, but with the guru.

The most common mistake you can make is to accept someone as your guru just because he or she can expound on some scriptures.

Your master must make sense to you, he must practice what he preaches and his teachings must be acceptable to you. Don't feel the pressure to agree with your prospective guru when you don't. Never take someone who curbs your questions or makes you feel stupid as your guru. In the presence of a genuine master, you feel important, loved and at peace; everything feels alright, life feels worthwhile. This is how you know that you are in the close vicinity of a real master.

You don't have to go in search of a guru. When you tread the path with sincerity and honesty, nature is left with no option but to manifest a genuine master in your life. If you feel guilty, angry, resentful or restless in a master's presence, it can only mean one of the two things: a. the guru is fake, or, b. you are not ready for him.

Above all, make absolutely no attempts to deliberately feel reverence towards any master. Surrender or acceptance can't be forced; either you feel it or you don't, or maybe you feel it intermittently. Either way, it's fine. If adoration doesn't come from within, give yourself time or get yourself a new guru. Faith need not be blind.

On a sunny Sunday, at the conclusion of a discourse, many members of the audience approached the master to clear their doubts or just to greet him. "Thank you, Master," one of them said, "I had my doubts at first, but now, I stand convinced that you are even smarter than Einstein." The preacher beamed with pride and thanked him for the greatest compliment.

Over the next few days as he reflected on the remark, he felt increasingly baffled. *What did the man actually mean?* he thought. He went through his notes to see what had he said so profound that someone deemed him smarter than Einstein. When no answer came forth, he decided it was best to ask the seeker.

The next Sunday he saw the same person in the audience. He asked him if he remembered his last week's comment. "Absolutely, I do," he said.

"Exactly what did you mean that I am smarter than Einstein?"

"Well, Reverend," the man replied, "they say, Einstein was so smart that only ten people in the entire world could understand him. But sir, no one can understand you."

If your master is too cryptic, he doesn't know what he's talking about. Truth is always simple, lies are complicated. If you examine the lives of the greatest sages, the realized ones, you'll discover that they preached in a way even a child could understand. Such simplicity only comes from experience, from genuineness.

When they don't make sense to you, chances are, they are not talking sense at all. It doesn't mean you have to agree or disagree with the master, but, at least, their words should be within the purview of your comprehension.

Once you find a master who walks the talk, whose presence pierces your heart, whose teachings transform you, whose words make you feel divine, don't let go off him, because he, with each unfolding moment, will elevate you even higher. You, then, will experience your own greatness, beauty and magnificence in your every thought. The pristine you then will shine softly like the full moon amid the night of emotions—both co-existing and complementing each other.

# BETRAYAL OF TRUST

---

A true guru's presence is like the soft stream that
gently sculpts the disciple, chiseling the rock of their
hardened tendencies. Steadily.

---

OFTEN I GET QUESTIONS around guru, the role of guru,
surrendering to your guru, how much should one trust his
guru and so on. A lovely reader who has been following my
blog for a while, and has already read my memoir, wrote to
me recently. She was greatly, and perhaps rightly, distressed
after reading an article about Satyananda (1923 – 2009), a
famous yoga guru, whose ashram is being investigated for
sexual abuse. She wrote:

> After marinating about this issue for some time, and after I
> read your memoir, I have some conclusions:
>
> 1. Guru is still human and not all of them are free from
>    samskara. Hence, the many cases of abusive gurus. Guru
>    is a position of absolute power and like George Orwell
>    said, "Power corrupts and absolute power corrupts

absolutely." True guru, clear of bondage, does not abuse this power.

2. Separate the teachings from the guru (emphasis mine). Despite of this issue, I still think the yoga knowledge they passed on is good. So, take the good, leave the bad alone. If Guru cannot give anything good anymore – move on. Like you moved on from Baba. Like Buddha moved on from his teachers Alara and Udaka.

I am in no position to comment on Swami Satyananda or anyone else. I don't know the details of the case or the truth in it. Yet, I am happy to offer you my perspective on the guru-shishya relationship.

I wish it was that easy — to separate the teachings from the guru. It's certainly not impossible, but it's not a breeze either. I am not sure if I can give you a satisfactory answer. Nevertheless, let me share my views on this important subject.

I've said in the past that the relationship between a guru and a disciple is like no other because it's free from the usual give and take. But, an important question to address is who is a guru or what makes a person a guru? Wearing the robe, completing a certain course, being able to meditate, or to be able to give a discourse, or having disciples does not make one a guru.

Anyone can don a robe — white, black, ocher or any other, it doesn't matter. Just like people study physics or English literature, they can study the Vedic or yogic literature too; there's practically no difference — one exposes you to one school of thought and the other, another. Anyone who isn't afraid of putting in the effort can be a meditator or an orator, for instance. Insofar as having disciples is concerned, you can find ample takers for any philosophy in this world. Even the most absurd philosophies, the dumbest teachers or preachers can garner huge followings. A large following has absolutely no connection with the quality of a guru. It simply means the guru is appealing to the masses. Even a potato or a pumpkin has mass appeal, for that matter.

Look at the most successful meditation, yoga or spiritual movements of all time where followers have devoted their entire lives to the guru, sect or movement, but how many have actually reached a state of enlightenment? None. (At least, I haven't met any). Ever wonder why? Let me tell you honestly, my first guiding principle: no one has ever gained enlightenment in an ashram, temple or monastery. When a guru tells you to follow his system for realization or heaven, they are fooling you. You deserve better. They can call it this meditation or that meditation, this *kriya* or that *kriya*, it doesn't matter. These are merely frameworks and systems, and they work because when it comes to spirituality, a lot of people are happy with very little.

If you are going to put someone on a pedestal because they deliver a good sermon or because they are charming or knowledgeable, your chances of getting hurt go up exponentially. You may be mistaking a competent performer or a good marketer for a guru. They will turn you into puppets, they will utilize you to further their cause and they will exercise control over you because you are letting them. And this leads me to give you my second guiding principle: don't accept someone as your guru just because they have bowled you over. Follow them only if you would like to be like them.

If your guru teaches you to stay away from anger but you see him shouting, he's a hypocrite. If you sense greed and selfishness in him, if you see him telling lies while he asks you to practice the truth, he's a hypocrite. When, even though, he preaches love and compassion, but, no matter what the cause, if his buildings, ashrams are more important to him than the well-being and welfare of those who look up to him, he's a hypocrite. Please wake up and open your eyes. Abandon him. Don't accept the wrong just because your guru is doing it. And  that leads to an extremely important point: what is wrong?

When what these gurus say is not what they do, it's wrong. For example, if Osho slept with a woman, I wouldn't call it wrong because he never said he didn't. If Ramdev did, however, I would flag it as misconduct because he says he's a celibate. So long as their actions match their words, I don't see a betrayal. When your guru is open and honest, they are not wrong, even if you disagree with them. At that time, you have the choice to stay or go. And, by open and honest, I don't mean they have to hand you their personal diary (unless they ask you for yours). If their actions or conduct doesn't sit well with you, move on. Because, not everything needs to be judged, and just like you, your guru, too, is entitled to have a life of his own.

Having said that, I can tell you what is wrong regardless of how liberal your guru may be or how spiritual the situation may seem. When people are hurt, abused, molested or mistreated, it's always wrong. Always. When you are asked to lie to your fellow followers for any cause whatsoever, it's always wrong. When your guru tells you his way is the only way, it's the biggest lie. When you see wrong, don't put up with it and don't just leave. Speak up. Learn to trust your inner voice. Not all gurus are bad, though. Even in this day and age, where many of them are crooks, there are plenty of honest and good gurus, too. If you walk the path sincerely, nature will arrange for a guru in your life. Take my word for it.

Before you accept someone as your guru, take your time. Examine him thoroughly. Repeatedly. Pointedly. Only take the person as your guru if you absolutely accept what he represent and want to become like him. Once you are ready, put your trust, not in your guru, but in what they stand for. Because, when you place your trust in a phenomenon and not just a person, when you invest your sentiments in a belief or a cause and not just its proponent, it no longer remains just trust, it becomes faith. And, faith, unlike trust, can never be betrayed, because true faith is unconditional. It's not based on anything.

Guru is not a position of absolute power but a conduit of unreasonable compassion. He will never abuse power because he doesn't hold any power to begin with, only love. A true guru will never tell you to tread his path blindly. Instead, he'll encourage you to find your own. He's gentle like the flowing river, warm like the winter sun, bright like the full moon, rejuvenating like the first summer rain. And, if you don't feel gentle, warm, bright and rejuvenated yourself in his company, he's not the right guru for you.

# Gods and Demons

---

If two bulls, one angry and the other one calm, are
fighting, who will win?

---

THE PURANAS — ANCIENT BOOKS of *Sanatana Dharma*, Hindu
religion — are replete with legends of *devasur sangrama*,
battles between the gods and the demons. In unmistakable
terms they also shed light on the secrets of body, mind, soul
and cosmos. They are full of stories of devotion and resolve,
of fervor and faith, of good and bad.

Most religions entertain the notion of gods and demons.
Even Buddhism, the quintessential path of meditation, where
Buddha tried to explain everything as a manifestation of the
mind, is not without the concept of Mara, the demon. Various
Buddhist schools acknowledge the concept of wrathful deities
like Yidam and protector deities like Tara.

The demon may be called *shaitana* in Islam, Satan in
Abrahamic religions, *daitya* in Hinduism or by any other name
elsewhere. A wise question would be, do they exist? Why do
they become more powerful at night, why do they feed on the
opposite of goodness? Have you ever seen a demon as religious

texts sketch them? In broad daylight? Allow me to shed some light on this.

Gods and demons represent elements of your inner world, gods are positive emotions and demons are negative emotions. Gods represent truth and demons represent falsehood. The former signify compassion, goodness and the latter indicate everything opposite of that. The demons may win some battles, even if temporarily, the war is ultimately won by the gods.

Similarly, in most people's inner universe, a constant battle goes on between the positives and the negatives, the rights and the wrongs, between the good and the bad. Sometimes, their positive side overpowers the negative one and other times it is vice-versa. At times they are able to overcome their anger and other negative emotions and sometimes such emotions overpower them.

Going back to the *puranic* legends, Indra is the king of gods and the Sanskrit word *indri* means an organ. It could mean either *jnana indriya*, organs of sense — eyes, nose, ears, tongue, skin — or *karma indriya*, organs of action — limbs, mouth, genitalia or rectum. Indra is not up there in the heaven somewhere, he is your mind. Your mind is the king of your body. It alone allows you to perceive and perform actions. Whenever your inner world is in turmoil, if your positivity outmaneuvers your negativity, your god wins, else, the demon wins.

The demon within you compels you to do evil and the god in you prompts you to do good. They are not two separate entities; they are simply two aspects of the same mind, like two sides of the same coin. Next time you find yourself getting angry, when you find yourself getting lured to do the wrong thing, remind yourself that the god in you is losing the battle to the demon. That reminder, that awareness, immediately weakens the demon.

Speaking from the meditation perspective, gods and demons draw their power from the same source — your mind. It is a shared resource. So, if you strengthen your positive side, the negative one wanes automatically.

A sage once asked his disciples, "I've two bulls in my mind. One is eternally calm and happy. The other one is always restless and indisposed. If the two go to fight, who will win?"

Some voted for the calm bull and others for the restless.

"It depends," the master said, "the one I feed more will win! Their victory depends on their strength. It is not necessary that one will always defeat the other. However, if you constantly feed the calm bull more than the angry one, it will grow stronger, its chances of winning every time go up."

If you ask me, it is truly as simple as that. If you feed the demons, they become stronger and emerge triumphant. When you boost the negativity in you, it will win over the positive you. Whatever side you feed gains strength, and the stronger tends to win.

Your method of feeding your positive side may not be meditation. It could be dancing, cooking, charity, chanting, praying, playing, anything — something you love. If you spend time analyzing yourself, you will discover your own method. In any case though, practice compassion and gratitude, they feed the calm bull. You will experience peace and strength.

# BEING AT PEACE

---

In the big scheme of things, no matter how much you have, it'll still be negligible. Peace is contentment.

---

MOST OF US HAVE a list of things we want in life. It can include a certain type of livelihood, a different lifestyle, maybe a different car or a bigger house, sometimes even different loved ones. It's not uncommon to see people wishing if their parents were like someone else's, if their partner was like someone else, if their life was different and so forth. It's not too bad to wish for something different, for, desires propel most people to act and live a certain way. So, is there a way to be at peace while living in the materialistic world? Yes. How? Let me share with you a little story first.

Once upon a time, a monk was giving a talk on gratitude. He was saying that everyone had something to be grateful for. That, we all had something of value, that, everyone was blessed by God. No sooner did he finish the sermon, a beggar approached him.

"I don't agree with you," the beggar said, "I'm homeless and I've no possessions of any value at all. I've nothing that will attract any price in the world. So, not all of us are blessed. Some are penniless and worthless, like me. "

The monk gave a compassionate look and said, "What if, I say, there's something you can give and be paid Rs. 100,000 in return?"

"You are joking. I don't have anything worth Rs. 100,000, but, if you think I do, I'll gladly give it for even a fraction of that sum."

"Are you sure?"

"Yes. For Rs. 100,000, I'll give anything."

"Well, I know someone who will buy a pair of eyes for that much. Will you sell?"

"Of course not!"

"How about your kidneys, your legs, or your hands?"

"How can I give parts of my body?"

"But, you just said you have nothing of value. The truth is there are many things you have that are of value; only that you are choosing to not factor them in. You are taking them for granted as if it's your right to have them."

This leads me to the point I wish to make: gratitude. Often, people think that their life ought to be a certain way before they can be grateful. A mistake. Instead, when you start being grateful, your life will become a certain way. Try it to believe me. Imagine it's raining pretty hard. Desire is wishing for the rain to stop and gratitude is carrying an umbrella. If peace is the seed of happiness, gratitude is the womb that carries it.

Don't we all have enough to be grateful for? Just look around and you'll see there's plenty you have, plenty of grace, blessings, plenty of things — some valuable, some priceless. With every breath we take, the least we can do is to be thankful for everything we have. Rather than allowing the endless wishes to squeeze the breath out of your life, why not see how breathtaking this life is? Why not take a breath and pause, reflect and appreciate life as it is? Gratitude is not a promise of the future but a commitment to the present.

Mulla Nasruddin's girlfriend asked for a solitaire but he refused. "Why Mulla?" she asked, "don't you want me to always think of you? Whenever I'll see the ring, it'll remind me of you." "Of course, dear," said Mulla, "but rather than the diamond, I would rather have you look at your finger without the ring. That will also remind you of me."

There you go. You can think about what all you don't have and be sad or you can look at what you do have and be grateful. Trust me, in the grand scheme of things, presence or absence of a stone, be it a solitaire or any other, makes practically no difference.

How can material possessions help you to be at peace, to be healthier or even more connected? I'm not saying that money is not important. It is. It can give a basic safety net, but, how much is enough?

Look at the ocean, how gigantic it is. It's no more than the size of your hand on the world map. Our planet is no more than the size of a tennis ball in our galaxy. Our galaxy is no bigger than a mustard seed in the universe. The whole universe is a tiny dot in the infinite creation. Therefore, the meaning of our existence depends on how we value what we have and not on how great our material possessions are. Because no matter how much, they'll always be minuscule compared to what surrounds us.

Peace is a choice, an option, a path. Being grateful is the easiest way to be peaceful.

# YOUR SPIRITUAL WEALTH

---

What is the boat that will help you cross over from turbulent emotions to an inner ocean of peace?

---

IN THE LEGENDARY AND epic *Masanvi* of Rumi, there's a beautiful, albeit a little immodest, tale of a pauper and a miser.

On a hot Arabic summer day, a frail and an old beggar knocked on a rich man's door in the hope of alms. Seeing his pitiable state, he was let in by the guards and asked to wait in the verandah.

As soon as the owner of the house came in, the beggar pleaded, "Please, sir, can you spare me a piece of bread?"

"What do you think," the owner scolded him, "this is a bakery?"

"Just one bowl of flour?" he asked with hope.

"Do you see anything here that tells you that this is a flour mill?" the miser mocked.

"Please give me even a leftover piece of meat," the beggar persisted.

"Get out of here," the miser shouted.

You think it's a butcher's shop?"

"Sorry for troubling you, sir," the beggar said while leaving, "can I at least have a glass of water?"

"Do you see a river flowing here?"

The owner ordered his guards to throw the old man out.

"Wait!" the beggar waved.

Before they could stop him, he rushed inside the home and began urinating.

Rumi continues poetically:

The owner, almost speechless with shock, shouted 'hey!',
'Since this place is clearly a ruin,' came the gruff reply,

'Where nothing is to be found of any worth at all,
It will at least serve to answer nature's call.

The message here I will make quite clear to you.
Since not a falcon, royally trained hunting to do,

Nor a peacock designed to please and charm the eye,
Nor a parrot gifted with speech that makes one sigh;

Nor a nightingale in the garden making lover's cry,
Nor a messenger hoopoe, nor stork nesting on high;

Then exactly what quality is it that you possess,
That anyone would wish from you to purchase?

While I appreciate neither the beggar's nor the owner's conduct, I quite like the message in the story. Nature is full of beautiful and useful creatures. It has trees, plants, birds and animals that serve a purpose in the divine and intricate play of survival and sustenance. Unlike a peacock, parrot or a nightingale, says Rumi, we have no special gifts. So, what value are we adding to the world? And, if we have not the heart to part with a tiny portion of what we have, then what good is our life?

My focus today is charity. If you take a somewhat mystical view then it's not even possible to do charity because whatever we have in possession is something we have taken from someone else. We may call it bona fide earning or a noble exchange, yet, the truth remains that everything we have is simply a private accumulation of what was already there in the society. I'm not suggesting that you are not the rightful owner or that you should give it all away, but at the same time, charity *is* a deeply spiritual act.

Charity is not just measured in monetary donations. Compassion, too, is charity as is empathy. When you help someone in any which way you can, you are exercising charity. It could be as simple as helping a lady stow her luggage in the overhead compartment on the plane, or giving that window seat to the child next to you. Giving a smile to the one who hurt you is charity, too, as is sharing your bread.

Interestingly, not surprisingly though, thesauri list the following synonyms for the word charity — compassion, kindness, sympathy, kind-heartedness, graciousness, consideration, concern, tolerance, leniency, etc. When you practice or feel any of these, you are exercising charity.

Charity is not an expense or a gift. It is your contribution to the society. If you ask me, it is every person's social and moral obligation. Besides, what you have stored in you can only be known from what you give out. Whether you have love, money, arrogance, anger, compassion or kindness, you'll give out what you have in you.

Just like you save money, bit by bit, every penny adds up. Similarly, every little act of kindness counts. Every small gesture of compassion boosts your spiritual savings. That's what charity is: it's your spiritual savings account. When you need peace and inner strength, you draw from this account. It is where your good karma is recorded.

A man who was born into a very rich family led an extravagant and self-centered life, rarely ever giving out anything in charity. From farmhouses to penthouses and everything in between, he owned many properties. When he died and crossed over to the other world, he was allotted a small cell to live in. He could barely lie down in there.

"There must be a mistake," he protested. "I was born in a mansion and had all the luxuries on earth. Why suddenly this pigeonhole for my living space? Did my good karma exhaust or what?"

"Well," the angel said, "we built whatever we could from whatever you sent us."

While your charity may not be funding your mansion in the heavens, it is certainly building your wealth in the other world. And by "other world", I'm not alluding to some celestial plane but your own inner world of emotions, your spiritual world of blessings. If you can't donate money, if you can't tithe, then consider giving away your old clothes, or something. If nothing, at least offer kind words to others. Be gentle.

Here's charity in a nutshell: help whenever, wherever, however and whoever you can, with whatever you can sensibly spare.

Make no mistake, charity is not an ordinary act but a position of immense privilege. Reflect on it and you'll discover what a blessing it is to be able to give something back to our world.

# DOES GOD GET ANGRY?

---

Is it possible that God gets angry with you and punish you for your sins and bad karma? If so, would he be God, really?

---

THERE ARE TWO QUESTIONS I have been asked tens of times. Recently, someone I have known for a reasonable time asked me:

1. I worship a certain deity. If I worship another form or explore other practices, will that upset my deity?

2. Can a guru be perfect? Or can anyone be perfect for that matter? Only the Supreme is perfect.

Here's what I think.

## Worshiping other forms

The same divine dwells in all. Krishna says to Arjuna:

समोऽहं सर्व भूतेषु न मे द्वेष्योऽस्ति न प्रिय |

Samō'ham sarva bhūtēṣu na mē dvēṣyō'sti na priya. (The Bhagavad Gita, 9.29)

Thus: I am impartial and homes equally in all and I am even with everyone. I have no personal favorites and I hate no one.

Your God is never going to feel bad if you decide to try different things. If He does, how can He be God! Do you think God is stuck in the dualities of pride-prejudice, good-bad, right-wrong? Duality is a trait of the unenlightened. Whatever helps you tread the path of truth and self-discovery, choose that fearlessly.

Exploring other avenues can give you a broader perspective. However, it comes at a price. Until there is self-discovery, going through many things dilutes one's focus, energies and devotion; it happens naturally. Your God is a product of your belief, *samskāra,* conditioning and thoughts. If you have made Him into someone who is crossed, pleased or appeased based on what you do or don't do, you may need to rethink, perhaps. You are entitled to have a god of your choice in "your world". It does not necessarily need to integrate in the framework of "the world".

## The Perfect One

Everyone is as complete as anyone else, just like each one is as imperfect as everyone else. If you believe that no one can be perfect or complete and that belief helps you become a better, stronger, happier person, you should stick to that belief till you know better.

My point of view is somewhat different on this one, but if I give you my answer, that will be conditioning you, however subtle, with my thinking. Ideally, the answer to this should be found and felt as a part of your self-discovery over the course of your own spiritual journey.

त्रिविधा भवति श्रद्धा देहिनां सा स्वभावजा |

Trividhā bhavati śrad'dhā dēhināṁ sā svabhāvajā. (The Bhagvad Gita, 17.2)

Devotion is of three types Krishna says. Such devotion is formed based on one's samskāra both from this lifetime and past, he adds.

If there can be a perfect painting, a perfect piece of literary work, food that tastes perfect, their creators may well be perfect I suppose, at least so in their fields. If for anyone the first three can never be perfect, how can there ever be a perfect human being for that person!

Perfection is subjective and relative as it is dependent on individual interpretation. Some examiners never hand out perfect score, many others, do so with ease. Self-realization is not about attaining perfection; it is about redefining it.

# Do Prayers Work?

---

The effectiveness of your prayer depends on
the depth and strength of your faith. You create
your own miracles.

---

IF THERE IS GOD, and if there is such a thing called Divine Grace, do you really have to do everything yourself? What is God's role then? Has He just sent us on the planet to toil, to struggle, without any help from Him, has He thrown the baby out with the bathwater and thrown in the towel, too.

God is the finest artist. His creation vouches for that. He may be the foremost scientist, but he is certainly not a trader. The concept of God boils down to individual belief system. He is a product of your belief, your faith, your devotion, your reverence, and if you allow me to put it, your conditioning. A Muslim, Christian, Buddhist, Hindu, or any believer of any other religion, have their faith naturally inclined towards what they have been indoctrinated as God. They derive greater strength from praying to their own god.

Before I get to praying and grace, let me just take a moment to split God into two, figuratively speaking, of course.

## 1. With Form

Followers of various religions have branded god, they have labeled Him. Many claim superiority of their brand over the others. Some are okay to try different labels, others are fiercely, sometimes fanatically, loyal to their preferred brand. An elaborate system of religion is passed onto them as part of their upbringing and they further their faith based on their inheritance. If you look around, you will find this is how most believers or theists operate. If taking such a route makes you a more compassionate person and gives you joy, there is nothing wrong with this approach; it may even be a good approach. When you believe God has a form, it is only natural to assign certain attributes to perceive and narrate that form. As soon as we put words around any experience, others conceptualize it. Such conceptualization, intellectualization, forms the basis of misunderstanding and misinterpretation.

## 2. The Formless

Imagine you were never conditioned by your parents, your teachers, by others, in school, in shrines... What would be your concept of God? Do you think you will feel attached to your present notion of God the same way? If not, would you pray the same way? How would you perceive His presence, His grace? The formless God is an important vedic concept. This school of thought encourages a sense of oneness, of non-duality, that, everything, everyone, is God, for, what has emerged from God cannot be anything short of divine either. Yogis relate their experience of *samadhi,* exalted state, to the union with the formless.

I reiterate, if your faith, however labeled, helps you be

at peace, increases your utility to the mankind, inspires you to lead a virtuous life, you can safely stick to your belief. However, if it makes you rabid, ties you down, clips your freedom of free thought, you may want to stop, take a deep breath, recess and reassess your position.

What about grace? Praying? Do prayers work?

Scriptures adorn God with fine adjectives, mostly in superlatives, as the purest, greatest, omnipresent, omnipotent, omniscient among numerous other epithets and monikers. If He was not all these, you would not need to pray, you could bribe Him, fool Him, entice Him. That is not possible though, how can you fool yourself, after all. He is in you, the basis of your existence. Praying is your way of self-purification, of gaining inner strength, of becoming worthy of his grace, of connecting with Him. It is one of the finest paths to experience Him, to thank Him, to be with Him. It is the path of surrender, of decimating your ego, of putting the drop back in the ocean, of offering your presence, your potency, your knowledge, your very existence to the Supreme Soul.

Grace is His style of connecting with you, answering your questions, protecting you, being by your side, watching out for you. Such grace in the form of wisdom may help you to walk the noble path, in the form of blessings; it may assist you in staying the course with your efforts and so on. Grace is not always getting what you desire. It rarely is that, and in fact, it is being exposed to what is right for you, it is helping you overcome the hurdles, to sail through the lows and remain even through the highs. Believing in the concept of grace can instill humility in you; during massive storms, a humble blade of grass remains protected, it does not get uprooted.

Grace does not mean that He can directly absolve you off your karmic duties and karmic debt. Why would He? Because you have pleased Him with your fervent prayers? Can a bank manager write your loan off just because you enchant him with eulogies, with flowery words? He can give you options perhaps, he may advise you to capitalize on any possible exceptions, but not much beyond that. God is not going to stop the rain for you, He will happily give you an umbrella.

Praying is your method of connecting with Him, and Grace is His method of connecting with you. When you call and say 'hello', that is praying, and when He answers back, that is grace; sometimes, he calls back later. If you insist on stopping the rain, it is merely an evidence of obstinacy, a sign that you are being selfish, not thinking about others who may need rain. It is not going to work. Instead, pray for protection. If your faith is unshakeable, He will source an umbrella for you.

In case you are wondering about my personal position, I believe in divine grace, in God. I rejoice in both the aspects of Him: with form and the formless. Regardless of the religion, when people talk to me about their religious or spiritual experiences, I feel equally joyous. If it makes you happy narrating it, it makes me happy hearing it. I have seen my deity, multiple times, I have experienced *samadhi*, tranquil equipoise, countless times and can slip into that state, anytime, at will. You can, too, if you are willing to devote time to intense meditation.

On a lighter note, here:

Mulla Nasruddin and his friend, had been adrift for five days, in a dinghy in the middle of the Indian Ocean, devoid of food and water. There was no hope of survival. They prayed, they cried, they swore. Nothing worked. They were counting their last, basically.

His friend began praying one last time, "O Lord! I have

been a terrible person my whole life, I was unfaithful to my wife, I abused others' trust, I told lies, I never prayed, I cheated, I ripped people off, I spent my earnings on gambling and liquor. Please, let me live, forgive me. If you spare me now, I promise I will pray every day for the rest of my life, I will never gamble again. I will also give up—"

"Wait a minute," interrupted Nasruddin, "don't go too far. I think I can see a boat."

Trading and praying do not go together.

Gratitude is a form of prayer. So is compassion. Being kind is praying, too, as is serving His creation. Begging God is not praying to Him. A prayer in the right spirit can transform you. If your faith is firm, your prayers can yield results. That said, praying is not a substitute for the right karma; virtuous living or righteous conduct is not an escape route.

The easiest way to experience His grace is to be childlike, to live in the moment. Watch a toddler who has just graduated out of infancy to know what I mean.

# THE COBBLER AND THE DOG

---

Here's a beautiful story, a gentle reminder about the
purpose of spirituality — to see divinity in everything.

---

SOMEONE WHO'S BEEN FOLLOWING my blog and discourses since
the beginning approached me the other day. He narrated a
heart-melting story. Here it is.

"Swami," he said, "the first thing I do immediately after
taking a bath in the morning is to light a lamp at the altar and
say my prayers. Other than incense and lamp, I also offer fresh
flowers. I've a small fenced area where I grow these flowers
with great care and love because they are offered to God. I
water them every morning and evening."

"While you've just come from the mountains, it's been
extremely hot here in the plains," he continued. "Due to the
intense heatwave, people have been staying as much indoors
as possible. Even dogs and cows run for shade and shelter
during the day and heat is already scorching soon after the
sunrise. If you step outside, you start sweating even at seven
in the morning.

"It was a Sunday and I had barely slept the night before

because of a power cut, so I started my day later than usual. At around 9 am I went outside to gather flowers for my morning prayers. Much to my annoyance, a street dog had made its way through the fence and was sitting in my little lawn. A hedge of flowers was partially destroyed. The dog had dug a pit creating a mound of earth nearby.

"With his tongue lolling out of his mouth, he was resting in the cool earth. I was as sad as furious to see the state of the lawn. Plus, I thought how would I offer fresh and pure flowers at the altar now. He could have peed in any corner of the lawn and I wouldn't know. I got really mad and yelled at the top of my voice and the dog ran away.

"I prayed in haste because I couldn't focus at all, and spent the next one hour fixing my lawn. I was in a bad mood throughout the day. Later that afternoon, I had to see a cobbler to get my shoes repaired. He was sitting on the footpath of a wide road. A faded and patched umbrella was tied to an old stick that was strategically stuck in the seat he sat on. A smutty and tiny workbench, that looked almost vintage, had countless engravings from weathering numerous cuts from various tools over the years.

"Alongside an awl and other implements, a whetstone lay nearby. And next to it was a soiled bowl with water. This is where he would regularly dip his sole knife and rub a bit on the stone to sharpen the blade. Sitting on my bike, I was feeling hot and restless while the cobbler worked slowly and patiently. He seemed unaffected by the heat or the noise.

"He was about to dip his sole knife in water when a stray dog sauntered in and started drinking from the bowl. The cobbler stopped and smiled. One moment I was looking at the dog and the next moment at the shoemaker. He was watching the dog with unearthly serenity and contentment on his face. Soon, the water was finished and the dog was licking the bowl.

"Without saying a word, he reached in his bag, pulled out an old plastic bottle and poured more water in the bowl. The dog was drinking again. The shoemaker, too, took a few sips from the bottle and put it back in his bag. Given the soaring mercury, the water must be more than warm if not nearly hot.

"After drinking some more, the dog looked at him, wagged his tail and sat nearby. The cobbler gazed at him lovingly out of his beady and compassionate eyes set in his dark and grimy face. The concrete pavement was too hot for the dog though. He got up, drank a bit more water, wagged his tail again and quietly left. As for the shoemaker, he dipped his knife in the same bowl and went about his business."

"I can't even begin to tell you, Swami," he continued, "that how ashamed I felt. There I was, an educated man who had been listening to your discourses for years and reading your posts and yet I could not see any god in the dog that spoiled my lawn. I chased him away like a mad man. I was upset beyond words. And here was an illiterate cobbler, who probably never read scriptures, nor prayed at an altar, yet he was far more spiritual than I could ever hope to be.

"I hear you say so often about seeing God in everyone and treating them like God, but when I actually had the opportunity to do so, I failed miserably. A shoemaker, on the other hand, was living your words; he was adhering to the scriptures. I feel so guilty and terrible, Swami."

"Don't worry," I said. "At least, you learned a lifelong lesson."

"No Swami," he cried. "Please tell me, how do I repent."

"Your awareness is your penitence."

"Still, Swami," he persisted, "give me something to do."

"Okay then," I said. "Put a bowl of water just outside your home for dogs and birds. And keep three rotis or slices of bread next to the water. Every day. For as long as you can."

His story reminded me of Saint Ravidas, a shoemaker by profession, who famously said, *"Mana changa te kathauti vich ganga."* (If your heart is noble, then water in your vessel is pure like the ganges). In a yogic and devotional sentiment, his verses in the *Guru Granth Sahib* say:

Tōhī mōhī mōhī tōhī antaru kaisā,
kanaka kaṭika jala taraṅga jaisā.
Ja'u pai hama na pāpa karantā ahē anantā,
patita pāvana nāmu kaisē huntā. (SGGS, p.93)

Tuma candana hama iraṇḍa bāpurē saṅgi tumārē bāsā,
nīca rūkha tē ūca bha'ē hai gandha sugandha nivāsā.
(SGGS, p.486)

You are me, and I am You-what is the difference between us?
We are like gold and the bracelet, or water and the waves.
If I did not commit any sins, O Infinite Lord,
then how would You have acquired the name, 'Redeemer
    of sinners'?

Thou art sandal and I am the poor castor-plant, dwelling
    close to thee.
From a mean tree I have become sublime and thine
    fragrance, exquisite fragrance, now abides in me.

When you realize God, you become humble naturally. Arrogance and ego flee you like thieves do in the light. You become an embodiment of goodness; you choose your words carefully. You weigh your actions meticulously. You check your thoughts artfully. You act mindfully. It all happens effortlessly, for you see the same Divine in everyone.

No matter how learned or religious we may be, until we feel the pain of other sentient beings, we are all alike — self-centered and self-concerned. And when the truth dawns, you realize that we still are all alike — eternal and divine. Only the perspective changes. Before realization, you see bodies, differences and outer appearances. After realization, you see souls, similarities and the inner essence.

You see God in a dog then, in flowers, in an ant, in everyone. Every time. For, that is the truth indeed.

# Faith in God

---

He rounds up his sheep before dark. Or does He?
Depends on the strength of your faith.

---

THERE ARE MANY WHO believe in God just as there are those
who don't. Some believe because they have not done any
thinking, many others, because, they have done too much
thinking. The same goes for non-believers, too. Purely from
the perspective of believing, of those who believe in God, the
focus of my present subject matter, they are mainly of three
types, as follows:

## The Hopper

The hopper is the restless type. He believes if his current belief
system has no answers for his questions, perhaps another one
would. He is in search of a panacea — some solution that will
give him peace. The trouble, however, is that the hopper is
merely jumping from one belief system to another. He has
not sat down to either identify the problem or ask the right
questions. He's like a window shopper. He is hopping because

he is restless. All his attempts to turn inward or practice devotion prove futile because he lacks the resolve and often morality, too.

The hopper wants an easy fix for some deep-rooted problems. Upon his adoption of any new system, he feels good, relieved and consoled. This is the "beliefmoon period". It fades away quickly before he finds himself in the same old boat, almost as if reality woke him up abruptly after a short dream. His restive tendencies and desires overpower him and out he goes again in search of another solution. The hopper has little chance of experiencing bliss, realization being out of question altogether, until he makes some amendments in his living, life, thinking, conduct and belief. Dry speech, tall ego, unbound anger and a lustful mind are the signs of a hopper. He wants to change without letting go.

## The Prisoner

A believer of a different type, the prisoner is more stable than the hopper. His stability varies based on his internal state and external circumstances. Such stability is not necessarily because the prisoner is a better believer, but because he couldn't be bothered with any cognitive pursuits, intellectual quests or spiritual conquests. The prisoner is called so because he is a captive of someone else's belief system. A jail in the form of a religion, a cult, a sect and so forth has been built for a believer of this type. He feels life is a sentence he must serve. He has a chance to live outside the jail but he does not revolt nor appeal. He accepts the ways of the prison.

A lot of people are simply prisoners of their respective belief systems. They dare not venture outside. Unlike the prisoners of the real world, these ones are behind the illusory bars. If you have simply accepted a certain philosophy or religion because that's what was offered to you, chances are, you are serving a sentence. You are living by the rules passed onto you. If must you stay in the prison, for reasons known to you only, at least play the jailer. It is a much better job, a better role. In the prison, one may paint prettier than Picasso or sound smarter than Shakespeare, one remains a captive still. The "belief-prison" is a product of the conditioned mind, and, can be knocked down only if you are willing to put in the effort.

## The Pet

Unlike the hopper, the pet stays at one place. And unlike the prisoner, he gets love from his master as well from other residents of the house. He lives in harmony. A pet is the one, who after finding his answers, settles on a certain belief system with love, compassion and conviction. He gets past the hollow arguments and dry polemics. Belief is a product of intellect. As long as one says, "I believe", it means they have not discovered their own truth yet. The freedom of a pet is restricted to the whim of the owner. The expression upon realization automatically changes from "I believe" to "I know".

Anything second hand cannot be knowledge; it is merely information. When we use that information and arrive at a conclusion based on our own experience, that is knowledge. The primary difference between the prisoner and the pet is the degree of surrender. Being a pet of your own home (intellectual discovery) is far better than being a captive of someone else's belief system. The pet naturally finds joy on sighting his master. In the system of *bhakti*, devotional service, a pet is the greatest you can be. However, I reiterate, my present focus is wholly from the perspective of believing. The prisoner maybe as established in his belief system as the pet, but the former finds no fulfillment; he cannot play around like the latter, let alone have the "master" clean up after him.

True realization consumes all beliefs that tie you down and condition your world. Your experience becomes your guiding force and your unconditioned self, your guiding light. You no longer have to either believe or disbelieve; you get the third choice — create your own belief system. You no longer move between the various sets of dogmas. Faith is a higher form of belief. Faith, when held onto with cent percent conviction, can do miracles. When you instill morality, purity, surrender and conviction in your belief, it starts to change from a dry intellectual doctrine to a soulful entity of faith. Besides, when you experience your own truth, all definitions become immaterial.

Go on! Be a pet of your lord or the lord of your own world. Don't settle for anything less.

# A Word on Surrender

---

Surrender is knowing that the trees can't always be green. It is seeing the beauty in the colors of fall.

---

LIFE IS FUNNY BUSINESS. The more we think we have it figured out, the more mysterious it gets. Like some fine magician, Life makes us marvel at its ability to pull off unimaginable tricks. It so happens though that not all of the surprises are adorable. Some can be downright cruel. And it is when life delivers an unexpected blow that your inner strength is put to test. It is at that time that life summons faith and surrender in the court of divine law to see if they will stand by you.

Does faith mean that we will tame life? That we'll dictate the terms? How dearly everyone wishes it, but that's not at all what faith or surrender has to offer. Why bother surrendering or praying to a God who can't fix our problems then? Let me share a beautiful story from the epic, *Ramayana*.

Rama and Lakshmana were wandering through the deep woods in search of Ma Sita. They came across a serene and inviting pool of water dotted by shrubs of fragrant flowers. Lakshmana suggested that they bathe in the pool and rest for a bit. The tall and handsome Rama took off his bow from his sculpted shoulders and plonked it on the soft ground. Hanging their quivers on their bows, they entered the pond to soothe their tired limbs. Lakshmana fetched delicious berries from a nearby tree.

A little while later, they dried their bodies and got ready to leave. Just when Rama lifted his bow, he heard the faint croak of a frog. He looked down and saw a small frog lay injured at the spot where his bow had been resting. Overcome with compassion, he instantly picked the frog in his gentle palms.

"Why didn't you let out even a scream, O little one?" Rama said. "Why didn't you call for help when my bow hit you?"

The frog chuckled in pain, and said, "You are my savior, Rama! The whole world calls out to you when they are hurt but who is left to look up to when you decide to hurt someone."

"I'm terribly sorry," Rama spoke like an ordinary mortal. "I didn't mean to hurt you."

"But I'm very happy, my lord," the frog said.

Both Rama and Lakshmana looked at the little creature with intrigue. After all, what was there to be happy about?

"The only thing sweeter than dying by your hands, Rama," the frog continued, "is to die in your hands. How lucky I'm that I'm in your hands while I breathe my last."

When I'd first read this story, I was deeply touched. I thought it so beautifully captured the essence of faith. Isn't this what surrender is about anyway? That there are things outside my control and that I agree to let nature or God handle those elements for me. Surrendering to the Divine or having faith in God certainly does not mean that no harm will befall us or that everything will work out the way we envisage. It simply means that we accept the fact that there are numerous things that we don't understand in the intricate workings of nature and that we are fine with it.

As a frog, I may not foresee or avoid a mighty bow landing on my back, breaking my bones. But it can't break my spirit, my faith, my surrender. The desire-less God certainly wouldn't desire anyone's faith or wealth. So, surrender is not to please any God. It is simply to strengthen and purify ourselves. It is to lead a life of love and humility. Feelings of love directed at anyone we revere is surrender in a nutshell.

# DEATH AND BEYOND

# An Uncomfortable Pause

---

Is death a matter of choice? Does dying a certain way
mean you will or won't get to heaven?

---

I ALWAYS TRY MY best to answer any question I'm asked, as
directly as I can. But there are some questions I'd rather not
answer. No, not that I don't have anything to say, but because
the truth is often discomforting for the questioner.

Last year, during my overseas travels, a couple approached
me for a private audience at the end of my discourse. I was
extremely pressed for time and wasn't giving anyone more
than five minutes. They weren't penciled in my diary in
advance. Yet, I asked the person who was assisting me to
schedule them in.

They were let in and the door was shut behind them. There
was no smile on their face; they came, sat down meekly, and
kept quiet for the first couple of minutes.

My inner voice said that they needed more time. Theirs was
no ordinary problem. I got up and told my timekeeper waiting
outside to set aside 20 minutes.

"Twenty minutes!" he exclaimed.

"Yes. Twenty uninterrupted minutes. Maybe twenty-five."

I took my seat again. Another minute passed and the gentleman began crying. Loudly. Somewhere, I knew this was healing taking place and I let his tears roll for the next couple of minutes. All this while, his wife kept looking at me quietly. She, too, was crying silently. Eventually, he wiped his tears, composed himself and heaved a deep sigh.

"Swami," he said, "we... we..." and he burst into tears again. They both were crying now. Getting up from my seat, I went up to them and stroked their heads, like a parent strokes a child's.

"It's okay," I said, "whatever it is, I'll help you deal with it. Your loss is irrecoverable but there's light."

"Oh, you know, Swami, you know everything." And they cried even more.

I let my hands remain on their heads and prayed for peace. They calmed down.

"Swami," the lady spoke. "It's the first time he's crying after five years. I had been worried for—"

"No, let me speak," the man intervened. "Today, I want to tell my story. It was my 50th birthday, Swami. I had two sons and two daughters. We all went out for a family dinner and had a great time. Everything seemed fine; we came back home. The next morning, my eldest son didn't come out of his room. We got worried after a while and broke open the door. He was resting against the bathtub, in his own blood. He had slit his wrist."

The man began sobbing again. I handed him the tissue box. He shared more details about the suicide note his son had left behind and other things that were going on in his life. They never went out to dine again or celebrate any occasion, he said.

"We are ardent Catholics, Swami," he added. "He never missed the Sunday service. He knew that suicide is a sin. He was a brave kid, why did he act so cowardly, Swami?"

I felt their pain. There is no grief greater than the grief of a parent who has to see their own child go before them.

"Everyone thinks we are responsible for his death," he continued. "I feel guilty. Was I a bad father? Why did he do this? He was only 24."

"Do you want to know the truth as I see it?" I said.

Or, do you want to hear what the holy book says?"

"We believe you, Swami," they said. "Give us 'the' truth."

It's true that most religions regard suicide as a sin. It's considered self-murder in Christianity. Hinduism, too, calls it *atmahatya*, self-murder. Scriptures in various religions refer to our body as a temple of God (1 *Corinthians* 3:16-17 or *The Bhagavad Gita*, 17.6). All this is fine (even though I disagree with the assertion that suicide is self-murder); the truth is, religions can be so dry and out of place in the face of real grief. This was not the first couple I met who had lost their child to suicide, and like every other such time, I didn't want to quote books, however holy or godly.

"Your son committed no sin," I said. "The cause of death can be any. We are all traveling on the same train. Each one of us has to get off at some station. Some disembark earlier. They break their journey sooner. That's what death is, it's a break, a pause, albeit a deeply uncomfortable pause."

"If you believe me then let me tell you," I continued, "I

don't believe suicide is a sin and I don't think it's a cowardly act. Your son is not in hell, he hasn't been denied heaven. His soul will simply find a new home.

"And you are not responsible for the death of your son. The idea to take one's own life arises from deep depression, it's the most devastating outcome of a mental disorder. Just like a doctor is not responsible for a patient's cancer, a parent can never be responsible for a child's death by suicide."

"Swami," the father said, "I had an argument with him a week earlier, but I thought we had made up."

"Was it the first time that you had an argument?" I asked.

"No."

"So, the argument wasn't the trigger or the cause. It was his own state of mind." "Your loss is immense," I added. "The wound is deep. It'll take a very long time to heal. No one can replace your son. But, by not living your life, don't you think you are doing injustice to yourselves and your other children?"

The energy in the room changed instantly. It was as if they woke up from a bad dream. Suddenly, they realized that by only mourning their son's death, they were denying the gift of life to their other children. It was a moment of epiphany.

"Oh Swami," he said, "I feel a big load is off my chest. You are right. We must live for our other children, for ourselves, for our Savior."

They both smiled. They looked at each other lovingly and then at me and laughed softly.

I think to call suicide a cowardly act is to severely downplay the illness of the one who has left this world. Their pain must have been so great, their despair so colossal, their path so dark, that the only way out they saw was to end their own life.

For that matter, I don't know of anyone who has never considered death a reasonable option, however momentarily, to end the endless sufferings of life. Only humans commit suicide. We have all these religious theories and we think that we have it figured out; that life is supposed to be a certain way. Life, however, couldn't care less. Every time it hands us the pink slip, we feel betrayed and lost. We think life is unfair (which it is), and, like the impatient child who wants a candy, we are eager to taste its sweetness again. We want to come out of our misery. We crave for an instant solution, hopefully easy, too.

Human mind is a strange phenomenon. In its cruel moments, it can make death appear more beautiful than life, more attractive than any dream. That still doesn't mean that death is a choice. Suicide is not a voluntary act, or a conscious selection. No matter how it appears, no one "chooses" to end their life. Given how difficult and miserable life is for most of the seven billion people on our planet, if suicide was a matter of choice, many would have gone for it wholeheartedly by now.

Suicide is a terminal disease. It is the final stage of a mental illness.

If you have persistent thoughts of suicide, then you must seek help right away. Feeling suicidal doesn't mean your life is bad, it means that your depressed mind has taken complete control of you. It means that your freedom of thought is under siege by your own mind. There is always a way to restore the beauty in your life and when death seems to be the only door, you are not looking in the right direction then.

A famous preacher was sitting in a park when he overheard a young boy telling his friend that there was no God.

"Come to my sermons," the preacher said. "I'll show you the path to God."

"Why is it, sir," the young one asked, "that even though horse, cow and deer eat the same stuff — grass, they evacuate differently? A deer excretes little pellets, while a cow turns out a flat patty, whereas a horse produces clumps."

"Hmm… I've no idea," the preacher said, amused at the question.

"I see," the young boy replied coolly, "don't you think it's a bit too much to say that you'll show me the path to God when you don't know shit!"

Shed your fears, your theories and your beliefs for a moment. Listen to your inner voice. Nothing or no one should instill fear in you or make you feel guilty. This life, this moment, this is it. This is the truth. Right here. This is the only heaven and hell. Since we are here, we may as well live it. Let's flow with the river of life. Whatever be your past, put it aside, let it go. Make your present so beautiful, worthwhile and meaningful that even death sits by your feet and begs you to stay a bit longer, because with you around, even death enjoys life.

Be grateful. Serve others. Take up a cause greater than yourself. And, I promise, your life will take a whole new meaning, an entirely new dimension.

# Mass Destruction and Karma

---

Natural calamities are not punishable acts but corrective
measures nature takes to sustain itself.

---

MANY WRITE TO ME wanting to know the role of karma — what
place it has in the events of mass destruction and natural
calamities like war, genocide, massacres, plane crashes,
earthquakes, tsunami, hurricanes, and so forth.

I do not believe that the law of karma is your answer to
everything, every occurrence. It is possible to retrofit theories,
to force a square peg in a round hole and cover the gaps with
some adhesive, creating the illusion of a perfect fit. But it will
only offer a temporary consolation, short-lived solace.

Before I address the big question, it is important to
remember that it is conditioned mind alone that asks questions.
The conscious mind coated by conditioning  rejoices in
calculations, in analysis, in exploration. It thrives on curiosity,
it feeds on inquisitiveness. There's nothing wrong with that. In
fact, it is this very human trait that helped our race to surprise

ourselves, to amaze ourselves, to rule all the other races; whether that is good or bad, is up to individual interpretation. Consider the following:

## 1. The Questioning Mind

Imagine, on the one side, having a mind that is endlessly asking questions; the same mind is addressing them, fielding them, dodging and answering them. That is probably how human intellect has developed over millions of years. It is like giving clay to a child. He keeps on creating different forms till the charm remains and then he molds all figurines back into a ball and leaves it aside. He may repeat the process till he grows out of it, till he is fascinated no more, till he gets another toy. Similarly, your conscious mind keeps you busy; it wants to keep you fascinated, keep you engaged. It gets tiring after a while. Just like physical matter, mental matter can neither be created nor destroyed; it can only ever be transformed. Intellectual satisfaction from one theory today may give way to another philosophy tomorrow. Einstein put it aptly, "You can't solve a problem with the same mind that created it."

## 2. The Quiet Mind

Now, on the other side, imagine a mind that is diving in an infinite ocean of bliss; it has gone quiet. It is alert, conscious, super conscious in fact, but it is not bogging you down with endless questions about some philosophy, some abstract theory you want to plug into tangible thesis. Instead, it keeps you focused, your energies channelized, escalating your awareness to an entirely new level. Your most profound answers will emerge from a state of quietude. In quiescence, you start to understand what is important to know versus what is more relevant; your answers will no longer produce more questions and more answers and more questions and so on. It will come to a stop. You have to experience that state to know what I mean. I can only show the path, your deliverance depends on you alone. It does not come from scavenging second-hand knowledge, it comes from a dawning of inner wisdom; it is the outcome of quieting your mind so you may see the real you. It is easier to see what lies beneath the water when it is clear and still.

I encourage you to tread the path of attaining quietude to experience a constant flow of bliss, you will get all the answers, more importantly, you will get all the right questions.

Onto the question now; let me segregate it into two parts:

## 1. Natural Calamities

Our planet has developed its own coping mechanism, an evolving ecosystem, a sustentative cycle; it is not dependent on the human race for its sustenance, and as such, does not see us any more important than an ant. It does not reason like us. If it did, we would be long gone. Acts of nature are simply corrective measures it takes to maintain its existence. Whether that involves spewing fire by erupting volcanic mountains, or earthquakes to cast off the anomalies, it does so indiscriminately. Like the dog that shakes off water after bath, like the snake that sheds its old skin, nature renews, realigns and rejuvenates itself.

There is a natural order to most things: when butter is brought in contact with heat, it melts; wonderful it is, it is not an act of grace or grief. For example, there may be no media coverage, no sense of loss, if a hurricane hits an abandoned island and no one is hurt, for, no one lived there. Explorers may seek answers, reasons, from an ecological, geological perspective. It is highly unlikely anyone will approach it through some esoteric philosophy, religion, through arcane laws, predominantly because a sense of attachment is missing. However, if the same incident takes place in a densely populated coastal area, causing casualties, we start searching for an answer in religion, philosophy, in divination and so forth. You may agree to disagree, but all religions, bar none, are mere philosophies; actionable items are called rituals. Great spiritual leaders passed on their wisdom and followers shaped it into religions.

## 2. Handmade Disasters

If I have my facts straight, every minute, more than 250 people die on earth. It is accepted as normal; it is standard mortality rate, they say. However, when a couple of hundred die in a plane crash, or, lot many in war, in crimes against humanity, we label this as abnormal; absolutely, it is. Yet, just because the scale is bigger, or because the act is concentrated, it does not mean there is an all-encompassing intellectual proposition to feed a satisfactory explanation. Searching for answers in a religious theory or some cosmopolitan philosophy is just as abnormal.

Behind most wars, most crimes, lies misguided human spirit of competition, of misplaced emotions, of misdirected energies. Such heinous acts remain eternally hideous, driven by greed for power, for lucre and for position. They are commissioned to satisfy ego and lust. They are murky acts of glorified ignorance, unmistakable signs of a barbaric mind.

Since, we have an evolved intellect, how flattering, we like to give ourselves importance. Somehow we feel that nature, God, other people, the world, must owe us something. We believe everything must have a meaning. Our life, our death, every incident, every phase, every occurrence, has to be supported by some intelligent answer to appease the insatiable curiosity of the conditioned mind. There may be theories, scientific basis, cause-and-effect and what have you, but that does not mean there is an absolute reason. Whenever anything undesirable happens, we want an answer, because most of us have been conditioned to believe that if you worship God, if you pray, nothing bad can happen; you derive your own truth from that.

# THE ROLE OF SUFFERING

---

*The lamp of faith diffuses the darkness of suffering. You begin to see what's beneath, what's around.*

---

IN SPEAKING TO NUMEROUS people on a regular basis, in going over emails from readers all over the world, I've realized that whenever anything bad happens to anyone, the first thing they experience is a sense of disbelief. While each one of us have our dejected moments of self-doubt and worthlessness, secretly though, most of us believe we are better than the average out there. Most people believe that they are more giving, caring than their partners, for example. Or, that they are better performers than their peers. So, whenever any untoward incident comes knocking on the door, the first reaction is it can't happen to me, I don't deserve it.

After a while, when you begin to accept that anything can happen to anyone, including you and I, another question starts to plague the mind: Why me? I get to hear so many terrible stories of suffering that you really are forced to question, what could have anyone done to deserve this in their lives? And whatever it was that they did, could it be not forgiven by nature or God or universe or whoever? The truth is, some questions just don't have answers. The law of karma, of attraction, of manifestation, everything fails at times. We are only left with some theories, consolations and probabilities.

In our unceasing efforts to not only experience joys, pleasures and happiness but somehow hold onto them forever, the only thing that actually seems to remain eternal is the opposite of these — suffering. You skip a few meals and body suffers from hunger, you skip sleeping for a few nights and you suffer from weariness, you skip resting for a few days and you become sluggish and so on. It almost feels that nature is unwilling to give any discounts whatsoever, as if it has no regard for individual preferences at all. Why is it this way? Why is suffering an intricate part of our lives? Before I delve further, allow me to share a story from the great epic *Mahabharata*.

After the Pandavas won the war, they approached Krishna to thank him. At the fore of such grateful people was Kunti, the mother of the Pandavas.

"Ever since I can recall, I've constantly bothered you with my problems, Krishna," she said. "For your grace and blessings, I've never offered you anything in return. Like a beggar, I have only taken and taken from you. I know there's nothing I can give you. You already have everything, you are everything in fact, so anything I offer will be like showing a lamp to the sun."

Clasping her hands, he said, "You don't have to thank me, I was only walking the path of dharma. I'm glad that you will be the queen mother once again."

"But, I'm still not happy, Krishna, because I'm afraid. Even today, I have not come to thank you. Instead, I've come to ask for one last wish."

Krishna stood there smilingly, looking quiet and keen.

"I've a deep sense of insecurity," she continued. "Constantly struggling, and battling with adversities, I lost everyone and everything that mattered to me. I've mostly lived in great fear because my fleeting moments of joys were far and few in between. And now that fate has finally turned up at my doorstep with a smile, I'm afraid that with all the happiness bubbling over, I may forget you. So, I beg of you, Krishna, to not take my suffering away because it has always made me remember you. I don't want to lose you."

In happiness or suffering, our prayers are not designed to offer God anything in return. What can we possibly offer? They are aimed to keep our bond intact with him. Just as a child cries for his mother, just like a fish jumps high on the surface but returns to the water, our suffering keeps us connected with God, with nature, with each other.

Although, no one wants suffering in their lives. Kunti didn't either. But in expressing her wish, she has highlighted the truth of human existence: suffering has a way of keeping you united with the source. By no means am I saying that we should go around asking for suffering (not that you would do it anyway), but I'm suggesting that perhaps suffering could be looked upon differently. Maybe like a season, a passing phase. *I don't deserve suffering* is a statement nature doesn't understand and *why me?* is a question it doesn't answer. Therefore, if we truly wish to get past a sense of suffering, we'll have to focus on some other dimension of it.

One such aspect is strength. The strength suffering gives us, happiness simply can't. The former stretches you while the latter relaxes you. Suffering is the scorching sun that makes us appreciate the cold. It's the chilly night that makes us want the warm sun. It keeps us real. If you believe in God, then suffering adds truth to your prayers; it infuses sincerity and devotion in your personal relationship with Him. But, most importantly, suffering keeps us on the ground, it makes us humble. And, humility, I may add, is the most important ingredient of a meaningful and contented life. When you go through suffering, something changes in you forever. You emerge stronger, wiser, more grateful and empathic.

Agreed that you don't necessarily have to invite suffering or lead a life of deprivation to appreciate life. Besides, suffering is not the sort of guest that needs an invitation anyway. But, when it does appear in your life, which it will invariably, you just have to be patient and deal with it gracefully. You can't fight with it or tell it off. You simply have to work on the opposite. In the dark night of the soul, you gently have to light the lamp of faith. Surrender is the wick and devotion the oil of such a lamp. Presence of suffering no longer pervades the whole room then, only some corners, some moments.

At any rate, let's be grateful, for gratitude is the antidote to suffering. It keeps you grounded, makes you strong even in the good times. Suffering leaves in the face of gratitude; they can't coexist. The pain may still be there, but the balm of gratitude gradually heals the wounds of misery. For, as the wise one once said, pain is inevitable but suffering is optional.

Let's not lose what we have in trying to find what we have lost.

# THE LOSS OF A LOVED ONE

---

Over time, ponds may dry up, but they don't disappear.
Getting over the loss of a loved one takes time.

---

SOMETIMES PEOPLE SHARE WITH me heartbreaking incidents of how they lost their loved ones. There are those who lost their son or daughter, a sibling or a parent, untimely or unexpectedly. Many a time, it is so gut-wrenching that even as an objective listener my eyes well up. The shock, the trauma, the pain is unbearable for them, almost like it would never heal. They ask me what they can do to get over the pain.

Death is inevitable. Everyone we know will die one day. All of us are on a train and each one of us must get off eventually. Some disembark sooner and others later than us. We know it is only a matter of time yet it can catch one off-guard, like someone emerging in front of you out of nowhere. When one is mentally prepared, when one sits in expectation, in anticipation, it becomes relatively easy to prepare for even one's own death. This is rarely possible though. We may get the time to prepare ourselves if the loved one is terminally ill but it still doesn't mean we have come to terms with it. The one who is gone is gone, the ones left behind face the greatest challenge, greater than the death itself.

Various religions offer different perspectives. Some promise rebirth, others, heaven, or salvation and so on. All those are theories. Their rewards of promises may inspire an individual to do the right thing while living. They may offer consolation to those left behind. Such promises remain as unproven claims though. Nothing beyond that. While on the topic of death and bereavement, I could quote you from the *Bhagavad Gita*, from the *Bible*, from Buddhist texts and the rest, but I don't wish to offer you consolation; it is not my aim to introduce you to some philosophy. Instead, I just wish to share my own thoughts.

First and foremost, I want you to know that you will never be able to forget them. Any efforts you specifically direct at forgetting them will only make you miss them a great deal more. This is the harsh truth. And why should you forget them? Would you like to be forgotten when you are gone? When you begin to understand and accept the fact that the departed one has a permanent place in your heart, in your memory, in your life, a subtle healing begins. Do not force yourself to erase them from your memories, to exclude them. Just let it be for a while, let nature take its own course, let it settle. Bereavement heals one over time.

Grief has two key elements, namely, shock and denial. When you lose someone suddenly, to an accident, for example, it takes much longer to get over the shock, primarily because nature did not grant you the time to get ready, to prepare yourself mentally. We slip into a state of denial and disbelief. That leads to an inner resistance. And such resistance leads to inner struggle, depression and melancholy. When you lose someone to a terminal illness or someone who battled for life for a long period before they passed away, the shock and denial is not any less, it is just of a different type. Either way, it is traumatic. Imagine losing a limb. no matter how dexterous or perfect the artificial limb, it can never match the original. The void created by the loss of a loved one can only ever be partially, imperfectly filled.

Acceptance is the key. I am not talking about accepting their death, I am referring to accepting the fact that it is painful for you, that it is hurting you, and that everything else is simply a theory. Allow natural healing to take place, allow your emotions to outpour, give yourself an outlet. You can't afford to have them bottled up; it will make you angry and eternally sad.

If you allow nature to help you absorb and accept the loss, you will find it easier to live without their physical presence. Just like happiness, like laughter and joy, sadness and sorrow are basic human emotions. These make us who we are. Do not curb them. Be natural, be yourself.

What do you do when you are happy? You laugh. Is it not perfectly normal then to cry when you are sad, when you are missing their presence?

A realized Zen master was seen crying at the funeral of a man. Most were somewhat surprised; they had thought the master had risen above the human emotions. It was an unusual sight to see a monk cry. A child went up to him, tugged at his robe and said, "Why are you crying?" "He was my friend," the master said. "I'm crying because I'm sad."

If their thought makes you cry, just cry; let it out. Don't hold it back. Some may advise you to focus your attention elsewhere, to go out, to forget and move on, etc. You can adopt any method, any philosophy, any theory that makes you feel stronger and better, but the truth is, you can't fake your emotions, you can't lie to yourself. The greater the number of memories you have with the one you lost, the harder it is to forget them. No matter how intense the heat, puddles dry up quicker than ponds, whereas oceans never.

How long it will take you to move on depends on whether your store of memories is a small puddle or a gigantic ocean. You are going to miss them on their birthday, their death anniversary, on your own birthday, on other important events, on small occasions. This is natural. Let it be. You may as well make them and their memories a part of your life. After all, death is the other side of life. You are standing at one end of the river, and them on the other; you are on this side of the horizon, and them on the other.

Horizons don't disappear nor the river of time ceases to flow.

Our emotions make us human, positively directed; they make us divine, misdirected, and they bring out the devil. Self-realization does not mean that you lose all human emotions. To the contrary, you become so compassionate that you could cry at the slightest pain of others.

"O Ananda!" said Buddha, "parting from the loved ones is inevitable."

# TERMINAL ILLNESS

---

All rivers merge in the sea, all small things become a part of a bigger phenomenon, it goes back to its source in nature.

---

WHAT TO DO WHEN one of your loved one is diagnosed with a terminal illness?

It is one of the most agonizing, most painful experiences — to see a loved one wither away in front of your eyes while you put on a brave face and watch helplessly. We are more fragile and more caring than we would ever know. The greater we care about someone the more their pain we feel in our own hearts. Is there any way to be at peace during this difficult time? Allow me to share with you a little story.

In the quiet countryside lived an old physician. He had been seeing patients for more than forty years and was known for his kindness, for making free house calls for the terminally ill. He always took his dog along whenever he visited his patients. The dog would wait outside the patient's house while the doctor went in to see the ill person.

On one occasion, a certain man had less than three months to live. He was scared of death and confessed his fears to the physician.

"What will it be like after I die, doc?" he said. "Will I be alright? What awaits me?"

The doctor stopped scribbling on his pad and put down the pen. He got up, opened the door and looked at his dog. The dog wagged his tail, and as much excitedly as triumphantly leaped towards him.

The physician turned to the patient and said, "Do you see this dog? He didn't have a clue about what all was in this room, on this side of the door. The only thing he knew that I, his master, was here. And, that's all he was looking forward to."

"That's how I see death," he continued. "I don't know what it's going to be like in the other world or this world once I am gone. I don't really know the whats, the whys and the hows about dying. Like my dog, I'm unsure what all is on the other side of the door. But, I do know that I'll end up by the feet of my master. And, that's all I need to know because that's all that matters to me."

I find this anecdote particularly beautiful. Ultimately, it boils down to living with grace and peace for as long as we have the chance to breathe.

Even if there's no afterlife, even if there's no heaven or hell (personally, I don't believe in heaven or hell, except the one on earth), it doesn't really matter because an infinite existence awaits us. All rivers eventually end up in the sea regardless of their course, all the drops of rain either merge into ponds, rivers, lakes, oceans or they are absorbed by the earth. If nothing, they simply evaporate and go back to the source. Either way, from infinitesimal they become infinite.

This is the nature of nature. Everything must return to its source in its pristine form. All tiny things merge into bigger ones and we, too, must return to our source one day. It's not about living or dying, it's restoration of our original state. The Vedas call it moksha meaning the extinguishing of all attachments and freedom from all fetters including that of body, elements and relationships. Death is not the end of life, but the beginning of it. The drop becomes the ocean and eternally transcends scarcity, struggle, fear and pain. An ocean remains unmoved, it does not dry up, it does not wait for the rain or sunshine. It exists beyond those shackles. Death is not sleep but awakening.

I have only slipped away into the next room.
I am I, and you are you,
Whatever we were to each other, that we are still.

Call me by the old familiar name.
Speak to me in the easy way which you always used.
Put no difference into your tone.

Wear no forced air of solemnity or sorrow.
Laugh as we always laughed
At the little jokes that we enjoyed together.

Play, smile, think of me, pray for me.
Let my name be ever the household word that it always was.
Let it be spoken without an effort,
Without the ghost of a shadow upon it.
Life means all that it ever meant.

It is the same as it ever was.

There is absolute and unbroken continuity.

What is this death but a negligible accident?

Why should I be out of mind because I am out of sight?

I am but waiting for you, for an interval,

Somewhere very near,

Just round the corner.

All is well.

– *Death is Nothing at All* by Henry Scott-Holland

Titled *Death is Nothing at All*, this is not a just poem but a beautiful sermon, I feel. Let's not make our lives too serious. Let's be merry, play, laugh it out. Nothing is worth clinging onto. Let nature roll. It is what it is.

A dying man was visited by the local priest. "Do you surrender yourself completely to the will of the Lord and accept him as your savior?"

"I do, Father."

"Do you renounce the devil and his works?"

The man didn't answer.

"I've come to absolve you. Tell me, do you renounce the devil and all his works? Say you hate the devil and detest him thoroughly," the priest spoke with even more rigor.

"Reverend," the patient said, "with the kind of life I've lived, I don't know where I'll end up. So, I don't think it's the time to make enemies."

A little bit of humor makes everything divine. Therefore, the joke above. Let's pray for a better world, with each one of us doing our part. Let's be compassionate, loving and giving. It's every bit worth it. Such a life becomes larger than death.

*Sarve bhavantu sukhinah, sarve santu niramayah |*

*Sarve bhadrani pashyantu, maa kashcid dukha bhagbhavet ||*

May all sentient beings be at peace, may all be free from diseases. May we see nobility everywhere, may no one ever be in suffering.

# YOUR KARMIC ACCOUNT

---

The Karmic Law: it's a merry-go-round. No matter who you are or what you are riding, it all ends up at the same place.

---

IN A SMALL VILLAGE once, everyone was indebted, materially. People earned their livelihood based on local trade. The farmer would buy on credit and pay the supplier upon harvest, the supplier would source on credit and clear his dues when he got his payment and so on. Everyone owed someone, basically. There was a hotel in that village, more like a motel. One day, a rich merchant from a nearby town visited them. He thought of staying the night there. He went to the hotel and insisted on seeing the room before checking in. The manager agreed and informed him that he would require a security deposit of one hundred dollars. And that, if he chose not to take the room, his deposit would be returned. The merchant saw no harm and put a hundred dollar bill on the counter. The manager called a bellboy to show a room on the top floor to the gentleman.

Barely had they started moving towards the room, the manager took the bill and ran out of the hotel. He went to the nearby convenience store and paid his outstanding dues of one hundred dollars and returned to the hotel. Further, the store owner rushed to the farmer and cleared his debt of the same amount. The farmer owed money to a private banker, so without ado, he ran to the lender and paid back his long-overdue loan. The lender owed a prostitute and he quickly got rid of his debt by forwarding the payment. The prostitute, in turn, owed the hotel for she had once used a room for her trade. To protect her reputation, she ran to the hotel, paid the manager, thanked him and went her way. By that time, the merchant came down and told him the room was not up to his standard. The manager handed back the hundred dollar bill and the merchant left.

No one pocketed anything but the whole village became debt-free. Everyone was relieved of their stress, their loans and debts.

Similarly, in the whole scheme of things, in the play of nature, the bottom line does not change; the grand total remains the same regardless of the volume and nature of the individual transactions.

If you have accumulated a certain debt, it is you alone who has to pay it back. Let us say, a certain bank manager is your best friend and you need chips. You cannot approach him with the argument that he has millions in his bank and therefore he should lend you some money from someone's account, from anyone's account. Even if he wants to help, he cannot do it.

Nature cannot give you what you have not earned just like it cannot take away from you what is rightfully parked in your account. It is impartial. You need to deposit before you can withdraw. What you do with your life, your actions is entirely your own responsibility. Each individual has a separate karmic account. It is immaculately maintained, there are no mistakes there. If you give someone grief because that is what they give you, it does not cancel out your transaction. You both remain accountable for your actions on an individual basis.

The law of attraction and the law of karma may well operate in tandem, but it is possible for one to do bad karma and yet excel at attracting good things. The reverse is also true — one may be a wonderful person and may still attract terrible things in life. Good or bad, that does not absolve him off his karmic debt, it does not get written off. It is dealt with separately by nature. It is for this reason that sometimes who you may call bad, they continue to flourish till their last breath. They can attract desired things in life.

Good karma may or may not give you success as you define it, it may not give you a life of material richness and glamour, but, without fail, it will certainly reward you with peace and contentment. In fact, you can only do good karma when you are at peace within. If you are happy inside, you will not hurt anyone with your words or gestures, you will only see beauty in everything and you will only melt their hearts doing even more good karma. If you are bitter inside, if you are angry, you will find it increasingly hard to heal yourself. Like the wounded lion or frightened snake, you may only end up causing more grief to the other person, resulting in even greater anguish for yourself. Happiness and good karma complement and fuel each other.

So, if peace is important to you, just know that it is funded by your karmic account. The greater the balance, more the peace. It is in a state of peace alone that one experiences any type of joy. Ultimately, why do most people work, go on vacations, dine outside, live a lavish life, wish for comforts? To enjoy, right? To be happy, to be at ease with themselves, with those around them, with the world.

If you are happy to shed some of your expectations, desires, if you are willing to be a little more forgiving, a bit more honest with yourself and others, you will find yourself at peace. If you can maintain that state under all circumstances, that will be self-realization. In that exalted state, you transcend all theoretical and intellectual propositions, your mind goes quiet and you experience an inexplicable flow of bliss. I say this from first-hand experience.

With peace and contentment as your armor, mindfulness and nobility being your mount, you win naturally; good karma happens effortlessly. You are a product of your thoughts, emotions and karma. You work on any one of these and the other two align automatically.

Your karmic transactions are your responsibility. It helps to mind your own business, especially if it is a sole proprietorship — the only permissible ownership structure in the law of karma.

# Conditioned Morality

---

Is morality absolute? Will you kill one person
to save five?

---

I AM OFTEN ASKED questions around morality. People want to know if this is right or that is wrong, if that is good and this is bad, they want to know if certain acts are moral and others immoral. What is good and what is bad, I ask you. How do we differentiate moral from immoral? Those who ask me such questions often even have strong views on morality. That is not bad, it may even mean they are clear about it. Although more often than not, their views are not their own. These ideologies have been passed down to them. Each generation tends to believe the preceding one had it figured out.

If you take a moment to reflect, you will find that not only your morality is conditioned, it is conditional, too. You may have principles in life but that does not mean your moral decisions are independent, rational and absolute in nature. Depending on where you live and what religion you practice, certain actions that are moral in your setting, may be immoral in others. Let me share with you an interesting ethical thought-

experiment originally created by British philosopher Philippa
Foot in 1967. As follows:

> Imagine there are two rail tracks. Five people are tied on
> one track and just one person on the other one. There is
> no time to untie them. A train is fast approaching. If it is
> allowed to continue on the current course, it will run over
> those five people. You are standing next to a lever. If you
> pull it, the train will get diverted to the other track and five
> people will be saved. However, your action will result in the
> death of one person.
>
> What will you do? Should you let five people be dead
> or kill one person to save five? What if that one person is
> someone closely related to you?

Furthermore, consider the following variations to this
experiment:

## Variation One

Imagine a trolley is hurtling down the track towards five
people. You are on a bridge under which it will pass, and you
can stop it by dropping a heavy weight in front of it. As it
happens, there is a very fat man next to you. Your only way
to stop the trolley is to push him over the bridge and onto the
track, killing him to save five. Should you proceed?

## Variation Two

A brilliant transplant surgeon has five patients, each in need of
a different organ, each of whom will die without that organ.

Unfortunately, there are no organs available to perform any of these five transplants. A healthy young traveler, just passing through the city the doctor works in, comes in for a routine checkup. In the course of such checkup, the surgeon discovers that his organs are compatible with all five of his dying patients. Should he go ahead and save those five sacrificing the life of the healthy patient?

In all the variations, one person is being sacrificed to save five. The moral complications are not straightforward though. Words are printed black on white, but life is not black-and-white. You really don't need some religion, somebody else, to tell you what is right from wrong, good from bad, because they talk in absolute terms whereas life is anything but absolute. If you get caught up in the absolute rights and wrongs, you will only end up feeling guiltier. Set yourself free. By no means am I saying you go around breaking rules just because they are there, but I am suggesting that you examine the rules you have imposed on yourself. The path of compassion is often worth it.

When you find yourself navigating through a gray area in life, listen to your inner voice. In the words of Fyodor Dostoyevsky: "It is not the brains that matter most, but that which guides them — the character, the heart, generous qualities, progressive ideas." Brain is a calculating machine. It has the ability to justify any act, any act at all. Ultimately, it will be your character that will give you the strength to stand by your own principles.

Conditioned morality is a calculative proposition — if you do this then that will happen, this is good because of that, that is bad because of this and so on. Unconditioned morality, on the other hand, is an original act; devoid of calculations, it is simply about living up to your own benchmark, moral or otherwise. And unconditional morality? That is mostly a misnomer.

Do not hesitate to be yourself. Set your own benchmark.

# THE FEAR OF DEATH

---

Water evaporates and it rains back, nature's play
continues. Everything in nature is eternal. It only
gets transformed.

---

ALL SANE PEOPLE HAVE it — the fear of death. Let me segregate
it into two parts: fear from an immediate threat and the fear
of losing life in the distant future. At the bottom of the second
type is not just the fear of ever-inevitable death but what if
life does not end your preferred way. The real fear is of losing
all you earned throughout your life, your relationships, your
wealth, and above all, you. Often the greatest attachment one
has is to oneself and death is about separation. Therefore, the
fear of death is one of the greatest; it separates the real you
from all that you thought you were.

Death asked Life, "We are simply the flip side of each
other, yet why do people love you and hate me?"

"Because," said Life, "I'm a beautiful lie and you're the
painful truth."

Last year, a young man, single and adventurous — let's
call him Krish — visited me in the ashram. Once, he told

me, during one of his treks in the Himalayas, he managed to reach the furthest accessible point, just a few kilometers away from the Indo-China border. Everything was snow-white. His guide led him to the cave of a hermit. They sat in the cave and the sage offered them to stay overnight. It was a clear sky. Irresistible. You have to spend a night in the Himalayas to know what I mean. Krish decided to camp outside for the night. The hermit warned him of the danger of wild animals around, a concern he immediately dismissed as ludicrous. The spirit of adventure can easily subdue sense. *Yeah right! Wild animals in this snowy region?*

*Even vegetation can't hold out here, let alone the animals,* Krish thought. However, the guide chose to stay inside the cave. He had a family to feed. His responsibilities required him to operate within the periphery of reason and sanity.

It was a magnificent night indeed and around midnight Krish pulled down the zipper of his tent to take a peek at the Himalayan sky. He had to blink a few times, however, and pinch himself to validate what met his sight. There it was, majestic as it looked, only a few feet away, a snow leopard glimmering under the soft moonlight. With his heart in his mouth, Krish pulled the zipper back up in the most silent manner. Suddenly, he became aware of all the elements his life rested on. He could hear his own breath, his heartbeat, his pulse, he felt saliva drying up in his mouth, not only could he feel but hear every passing moment. The wild cat, lithe and light, faint and fierce, approached the tent and began circling around, as if circumambulating its prey in some sacred tribal ritual before sacrificing it.

"Those thirty minutes, Swami," Krish said to me, "were like a lifetime. I could feel the sweat in that icy cold night. I could understand how good meditation brings crystal awareness of absolutely everything around you. Admittedly, this understanding came after the leopard was gone. Never earlier in my life had I realized the real duration of thirty minutes."

You know what else gives you that experience of razor sharp awareness? Solitude. Minus the fear, of course. The feline animal went for a different meal leaving Krish behind while he meditated on that leopard for the rest of the night. There was no effort in that meditation. Krish sat there still. He felt no pains, no aches. Fear had conquered them all. He wanted to sleep, he wanted to think of different things, but the fear reigned supreme; he could only think about the object of his fear. Human nature.

Fear is our oldest acquaintance and it is easily recognized. Like with their possessions, humans have attachment to their fears, too. To be fair, probably anyone in his situation would have spent the remaining night in much the same manner. His pants remained dry, that was brave enough I thought. By the way, Krish is very dear to me and I find him an amazing individual.

Fear of anything is greatly dependent on our outlook towards it. If we change our perspective, the nature of the fear changes, too. If you start to look upon death as a mere pause and not as an abrupt end, you may even begin to like it, much less loath it. Think about this: once you cross the chasm of death, you will get another chance at life, another childhood, another youth, one more chance at living, at loving, at being.

Yes, death. Death must be so beautiful. To lie in the soft brown earth, with the grasses waving above one's head, and listen to silence. To have no yesterday, and no to-morrow.

_ _ forget time, to forget life, to be at peace. You can help me. You can open for me the portals of death's house, for love is always with you, and love is stronger than death is. (Oscar Wilde, The Canterville Ghost)

Nothing is dying or taking rebirth. Don't let the illusion fool you. Simply, the matter is transforming. Water evaporates and it rains back. Everything in the play of nature remains a part of the game. Eternally. There are no exceptions nor exclusions. Only the roles change, only the shapes vary. The sum total remains the same. You are an eternal being, an ocean of bliss. Oceans don't dry up. Drop your fears, live every moment. Rejoice. What are you clinging on to? Non-attachment leads to no-fear. How absurd it is to be afraid of the final destination of life. If we are scared of the destination, how can we possibly enjoy the journey?

No matter what your belief, irrespective of whether or not you believe in afterlife, rebirth or reincarnation, the real you remains the immutable soul. When you are sleeping and you are not aware of yourself, it is. When you are unconscious for any reason and have no knowledge of yourself, it does. Why you connect with some people just upon hearing their name even though you may have never met with them, because of it. It is the linchpin of all life, the string in the pearl-necklace, the fragrance of the rose, the heat in the fire, the cold in the ice, the essence of all phenomena, the warmth in the heart, the emotion in your tears, 'it' is your atman, the soul. Indestructible. Indivisible. Complete. Unfathomable. Unknowable.

Rethink about your life. Rewrite your rules. About time.

Made in United States
North Haven, CT
23 February 2023

33037555R00133